Table Of Contents

Acknowledgments

The call to collect mystical stories for this book came in the fall of 1999 after hearing Todd Chrisler and Roy Nelson tell of dramatic mystical experiences in their lives (see chapters 2 and 3). I remembered several other people who had told of such experiences over my thirty years of pastoral ministry. It occurred to me that there must be many others with such revelations to share, if only someone would ask. I started to ask everyone I saw. Many people nodded knowingly and told of the presence of God in their lives, of a vision, of a direct audible answer to prayer, of an aroma that could only have been from beyond, of a healing, of an angel visitation, of a dream or an appearance of a deceased loved one that brought comfort, indescribable joy, and peace. And, often I heard the words, "I've never told anyone about this before."

I want to thank the 65 contributors to this collection for trusting me with their sacred stories. Hearing and recording these powerful, life-changing experiences has enriched my life beyond measure.

I am grateful for the spiritual guidance and encouragement of Jacquelyn Oliveira, Lisa Mohr, Kendall Anderson, Kerri Sherwood, Mary Peterson, Carol Smith, Brad Van Fossen, Steve Fringer, Jim and Marianne Cotter, Jo Bierer, June Nettles, Lois Grebe, Susan Leih, Sung Keun Kim, Bill Morton, J. Wesley Corbin, David Heckenlively, Thomas Moe, Sharon Zimmerman Rader, Velma Smith, and my friends in the "Three Year Covenant Community": Bruce Stunkard, Ann Peterson, Wendy Wosoba, Martha Macias, Diana Lampsa, Gerry Harrison, David Guse, Theonia Amenda, David Sharpe, Patricia Zealley, Jacqueline Baumgart, and Patricia Lietzke.

I owe more than I can ever repay to my research assistant, Rebecca Henderleiter, who made phone calls, researched leads on the Internet, interviewed prospective contributors, transcribed tapes, and wrote two wonderful stories of her own mystical experiences.

The book would not have been possible without the many contributions of the love of my life, Jo Perry-Sumwalt, who assisted

9

me with the editing, typed the manuscript, dreamed the book with me on our early morning walks, and tolerated my endless ruminations about the meaning of it all. We are both grateful for the loving support of our children, Kathryn and Orrin.

Advent

Some people claim that mystical visions are occurring more frequently because we, as a species, are evolving, so that what was once the province of a few saints is now our common heritage ... I write in case others have had such experiences and want to know they are not alone.

Sophy Burnham

Sophy Burnham, *The Ecstatic Journey: The Transforming Power Of Mystical Experience* (New York: Ballantine Books, 1997), p. 5.

A Safe Place To Tell Visions

John Sumwalt

*O that you would tear open the heavens and come
down so that the mountains would quake at your
presence.* (v. 1)

Late on Maundy Thursday evening, in the year 2000, as I lay
in bed, meditating on the format of this book, a thought came into
my head that I would be able to see a spirit if I simply looked. I
opened my eyes and saw something indescribably beautiful about
two feet above my head. It was a bright, luxurious purple, then
deep azure blue, radiant, dynamic, pulsating: a being of light and
energy moving slowly closer and closer. As it drew near, I tried to
communicate through thoughts, asking who or what I was seeing,
and the meaning of the visitation. There was no discernable response. Then the spirit touched me, more like flowed into my being. I felt warmly loved. The warmth moved over and through my
body like liquid energy. It was exhilarating, like nothing I have
ever experienced before. The vision lasted three or four minutes.

The memory of this encounter with the holy still warms my
heart. I continue to experience it as a healing presence. I am healthier
physically, emotionally, and spiritually than I was before I opened
my eyes that night. Most of the painful symptoms of a debilitating
illness I had suffered periodically for seven years have abated. The
vision is a "blessed assurance" of the presence of God, an answer
to prayers for healing, and a beacon to light my way in the years to
come. I am grateful beyond words.

What I can express about my vision I have learned to say carefully to persons I have reason to believe might be receptive. Some
people don't know what to say when they hear of an experience
like this. Others dismiss it as foolishness. We live in a culture that

is not vision friendly. Eddie Ensley, a Roman Catholic writer of Native American descent, writes in his book, *Visions: The Soul's Path To The Sacred*: "Talk of visions went underground, at least in polite company, with the rise of modern science in the sixteenth and seventeenth centuries." Yet, he says, people have visions all the time. Ensley tells of a survey of 2,000 Christians in mainline churches in St. Cloud, Minnesota, which found that thirty percent had seen dramatic visions, heard heavenly voices, or experienced prophetic dreams. Ensley adds, "Almost every one reports some partly remembered sacred moment — once they feel secure enough to talk about it."[1]

Many people have had this kind of life-changing experience, but have never felt safe enough to tell anyone. Susan Andrews, pastor of Bradley Hills Presbyterian Church in Bethesda, Maryland, tells of a widowed parishioner whose eyes filled with tears as she spoke to her in the Fellowship Hall one Sunday after worship.

> *"Bob came back and crawled into bed with me. He didn't say a word. He just appeared — and then faded away. I felt immediate peace and warmth and hope, and now I don't feel alone." Then glancing up in pink but eager embarrassment, she asked, "You don't think I'm crazy, do you?"*[2]

A few months after I had shared this story in a sermon, I went to the hospital to visit Mavis Meyer, a member of our church, who had received word the night before about the death of a favorite niece. I listened as she poured out her grief, and then as an afterthought, asked her if she had had any sense of her niece's presence since her passing. She looked at me knowingly and said, "Not yet, but after my husband died, six years ago, he was often in my bedroom at night. One night, after I had been in bed for awhile, trying to sleep, I opened my eyes and there was my husband and my late stepson hovering over me. I was so startled that I exclaimed, 'Go away!' " We both laughed, and then she told me that she had never spoken of this to anyone before.[3]

Marjorie Thompson writes about a woman she knows who had a profound encounter with the holy when she was fourteen.

> The voice said, "You are my beloved child; walk with me, and you will heal many people." She felt flooded with a sense of well-being and peace and was powerfully moved to serve God. Yet until we met, she had never felt free to share her experience with anyone in her family or church.[4]

Who would you tell if this happened to you? Would you feel safe telling your family or your friends at work? Could you confide in your physician, your pastor, or the people you worship with at church? In spite of the many mystical stories we know in scripture, and over two centuries of mystic lore handed down by a multitude of saints and sinners, we moderns do not feel comfortable telling about such visitations in church or anywhere else. We live in an age in which most of us have been schooled to be skeptical of anything that cannot be verified scientifically. This means many of us keep silent about some of the most profound experiences of our lives, lest we be accused of being delusional.

Ross Oestreich, a clergy colleague who was on a board responsible for interviewing seminarians seeking ordination in our denomination, remembers a student who fled the meeting when pressed for more candor about his call to ministry. Ross said, "When I found him later, in the basement of one of the dormitories, he told me he dared not tell of his experience with God, because we would think he was crazy. I invited him to try sharing with me. I did not think he was crazy. I resonated with some of his experiences. He had a master's degree in psychology and had been an instructor in that field in a small college before entering seminary." Ross said, "What I found troubling was his assumption that a group of clergy would think he was crazy for having spiritual experiences. I could understand his fear to tell such experiences in a group of persons in the field of psychology. Why was it not safe to tell clergy? Thirty years later, I am still troubled by his comments."[5]

What if Moses had never told anyone about the burning bush? What if Samuel had not run to someone who understood that it was God who was calling his name? What if Paul had kept quiet about his vision of Christ on the road to Damascus, or if John had never written a word of what he saw during his exile on the island of Patmos? Much of our Christian heritage comes from the told visions of faithful followers of Jesus who were willing to risk ridicule, and in some cases persecution and death, to give witness to the presence of God in their lives. What if, after reading this, you are visited by an angel or a loved one who comes to bring you a blessing from heaven? Who are you going tell?

Renita Weems tells how fortunate she was to have had someone to tell who understood the strange night vision she experienced in her bedroom at the age of seventeen. Two people appeared and sat on the empty bed across the room, whispering to each other and noisily thumbing through the pages of a book. They never looked at her, but communicated with her all the while they were there. Weems ran downstairs and woke her stepmother:

> *She heard me out ... and without appearing the least bit surprised or flabbergasted by the dream, assured me that the people in my dream were probably angels coming to tell me something.*[6]

In March of 2001, I offered a series of five Lenten classes at our church titled *A Safe Place To Tell Visions*. Each week, I gave a reading assignment which included vision stories from scripture, selected chapters from Eddie Ensley's book, *Visions: The Soul's Path To The Sacred* and Jacquelyn Oliveira's book, *The Case For Life Beyond Death*. I also showed very brief excerpts from movies that include visions. Among these were *The Messenger* (the story of Joan of Arc), *The House of Spirits* (based on Isabelle Allende's novel of the same title), *The Milagro Beanfield Wars*, *Field of Dreams*, *What Dreams May Come*, and *Always*.

Near the end of each class, I announced a time for telling visions. Some of the stories in this collection were revealed during this time. I have discovered over the years that, wherever eight to ten people are gathered, and a vision story is told, two or three others in the group will tell a similar story. Almost everyone has a personal vision story to tell, or knows the story of a friend, and will share it if they know that the sacredness of the story will be honored. It is my hope that, as the stories in this book are read and told, many more faithful souls will find a safe place to tell their visions.

---

1. Eddie Ensley, *Visions: The Soul's Path to the Sacred* (Chicago: Loyola Press, 2000), pp. 12-13.

2. Susan R. Andrews, "Jesus Appears," *The Christian Century*, March 1999, p. 341.

3. Mavis Meyer is a longtime member of Wauwatosa Avenue United Methodist Church in Wauwatosa, Wisconsin.

4. Marjorie J. Thompson, *Soul Feast: An Invitation to the Christian Spiritual Life* (Louisville: Westminster John Knox Press, 1995), p. 4.

5. Ross Oestreich is a recently retired United Methodist pastor who lives in Sun Prairie, Wisconsin.

6. Renita J. Weems, *Listening for God: A Minister's Journey Through Silence and Doubt* (New York: Simon & Schuster, 1999), p. 99.

Jacquelyn Oliveira's book, *The Case for Life Beyond Death*, can be ordered from William Laughton Publishers, P.O. Box 588, Elm Grove, Wisconsin 53122-0588. Phone 1-800-686-1250.

Cameron's Story

Todd Chrisler, as told to John Sumwalt

Then the glory of the Lord shall be revealed, and
all people shall see it together, for the mouth of
the Lord has spoken. (v. 5)

I met Todd and Dawn at wedding reception in the fall of 1999. They disclosed, very cautiously, that they had lost a child to cancer in 1998. The following day was to be the anniversary of their eight-month-old son's death at a nearby hospital. Todd told me about the anguish of their last 24 hours with Cameron: of chemotherapy, numerous tubes, blood transfusions, and endless tests. The doctors had told them there wasn't much hope. They were in a small sleeping room next to the intensive care unit, trying in vain to sleep. Todd said he was praying for God to be with Cameron, to end his ordeal, to give him peace, when he noticed thoughts coming into his mind that were clearly not his own. "Cameron is going to be with me. He is going to be cared for. I will take Cameron at 5:38."

Todd wondered if he was having a dream, if what he was being told was real or only his imagination. He reached over and roused Dawn, who was dozing, and whispered, "5:38, 5:38, remember 5:38." She asked, "What?" and he told her just to remember that number. Dawn told him later that she had understood exactly what he meant. Then, Todd said, a feeling of calm came over him. The overwhelming stress and anxiety he had been feeling were gone. It was like a burden had been lifted off his chest. The next morning he awoke, rested, at about 9:30 a.m. When he realized that 5:38 had passed, he felt let down again, thinking he must have imagined the whole thing. Todd and Dawn continued the vigil with heavy hearts.

Late in the afternoon, their beloved child, who had been unresponsive for days, opened his eyes, looked at them, and then closed his eyes for the last time. After consulting with the doctors, they made the decision to disconnect Cameron from all of the machines. They held him in their arms as he died, and said their good-byes. Then Todd and Dawn went back into the sleeping room to collect their things. Suddenly they realized that they had been holding Cameron at 5:38 p.m. when he died, just as God had told them. They left the hospital with a feeling of peace, knowing that God had been with them and had blessed them in their hour of need.

To Bind Up The Broken Hearted

Roy H. Nelson, as told to John Sumwalt

*The Spirit of the Lord is upon me, because the Lord
has anointed me; he has sent me to bring good
news to the oppressed, to bind up the broken
hearted, to proclaim liberty to the captives, and
release to the prisoners ... to comfort all who
mourn, to provide for those who mourn in Zion —
to give them a garland instead of ashes, the oil of
gladness instead of mourning, the mantle of praise
instead of a faint spirit.* (vv. 1-3a)

Roy Nelson, an attorney, who is a member of St. Matthew's
Lutheran Church next door to the church I serve in Wauwatosa,
told me of the unrelenting grief and depression he experienced after his wife's death from cancer at the age of 33. They had been
married eleven years and she was the center of his universe. For
months after Gail's death, in July of 1993, Roy felt numb and empty.
He was seeing a pastoral counselor twice a week, but nothing
seemed to help. Following Christmas, Roy said, he sank even lower,
and wondered, "What is going to become of me?"

Then, he said, "One night as I knelt beside my bed, thinking
that nothing really mattered and believing I could not bear the crush-
ing burden of my grief, the thought came to me, 'If I ask God to
carry my burden, God will.' " I admitted to God I couldn't do it on
my own and called on God to take up my burden of grief and sor-
row, and carry it for me so that I could get out from under it. My
arms were lifted up to the sides and slightly in front. It wasn't vol-
untary. I did not do it. It wasn't any effort to hold them there. I felt
something like electricity flowing from my heart, out of my chest,
up through my arms, out my finger tips, and even out of the top of
my head. I thought I must be deceiving myself. I thought, "This

can't really be happening." Then a voice way in the back of my head said, "Don't doubt now, because this really is happening." I caught myself saying out loud, "God, I do believe. I know it's you doing this. I know you are helping me; you are doing what I asked you to do. I do believe! I don't doubt!" And this process continued, this sensation of electricity coming out of my fingertips and out of the top of my head. I felt the burden being lifted. It didn't take very long, five minutes or so, and then my arms were lowered back down. I knelt there awestruck, absolutely awestruck that God cared so much about me, individually, that he would take my burden from me. The heaviness of the grief and depression was gone. I then felt something I had never felt in my life before: a peace and contentment being poured down through my head and filling my chest, filling my heart. I thought, 'This must be the peace of God. Thank you, God.' "

Roy says he still asks God to lift his burdens from time to time, and God does. Shortly after his healing experience, Roy met a marvelous woman who was singing in their church choir. Roy and MaryJean were married in August of 1994, and have two children. As of this writing, Roy is preparing to enter seminary.

What Is God Saying?

Susan D. Jamison

And he came to her and said, "Greetings, favored one! The Lord is with you." But she was much perplexed by his words and pondered what sort of greeting this might be. (vv. 28-29)

In May of 1996, I attended an event at Kirkridge, located in the Pocono Mountains of Pennsylvania. I had known of this retreat center for about ten years, had received their catalogs of events, but had not found the time and money to go there. But this event was too good to pass up: a weekend of dancing and drumming. This was the first time I had ever attended an event where I would use my body, instead of my intellect, to learn. Once there, the staff encouraged us to visit Columcile, a sacred space that included megalith stones, built by a retired Presbyterian minister about 25 years ago.

The grounds of Columcile touch the grounds of Kirkridge, but I had never heard of it before. Early Sunday morning I decided to visit Columcile, although I had no idea what to expect. As I approached from Kirkridge, I saw an arched stone entrance and passed beneath it. A short path led me downhill past some large rocks to a small stream. At the bridge across the stream, I looked up the hill, where the path continued, and saw a stone chapel. I began to tremble at the sight, for I knew I had seen that chapel, had been inside it, even though I had never physically been in this place before. I walked up the hill, and, with trembling hands, opened the door of the chapel and stepped inside. It wasn't exactly as I remembered, but close. I sat down on one of the benches against the wall, closed my eyes, and remembered.

About ten years before my introduction to Columcile, I had gone on a one-day retreat for United Methodist clergywomen in

Central Pennsylvania. Our retreat leader led us in a guided meditation. I am not usually successful at this, finding it too difficult to focus, with too many distractions and an inability to concentrate. But this time I was able to quiet my mind and really enter into the process. We were asked to envision a field of grass and wild flowers, to feel the warmth of the sun on our faces and be totally relaxed. Then we were invited to imagine a path leading out of the field, up a hill.

"What is at the top of the hill?" the leader asked. I saw a six-sided chapel, made of large stones, with a peaked roof. There were tall, narrow, arched windows in each side. We were encouraged to walk up the hill and just be with whatever we found. In my mind, I walked up the hill and into the chapel. There were a few pews arranged to face an altar, and light shone dimly through the thick glass windows. I sat on one of the pews in the dark, cool quietness.

"What is God saying to you here?" she asked. As I sat there, a wispy, white presence came into my line of vision and floated up toward the ceiling. I distinctly heard the words, "Take time to rest. You are loved."

At that time of my life, I was working full-time as a parish pastor, had a two-year-old, and was married to a pastor who was a workaholic. I was exhausted physically, emotionally, and spiritually. I felt such a sense of peace, sitting in that chapel, surrounded by the presence of God. Ten years later, sitting in this chapel that was so familiar and so comforting, I had to acknowledge that something mystical had happened to me all those years before. I had been in *this* chapel in that guided meditation. I don't understand it, but somehow I had!

And so I asked myself, "What is it that God is saying to me, here, now?" I was, at that time, struggling with whether or not to leave an unhealthy marriage, and with whether or not I wanted to stay in parish ministry or go back to school. I was just beginning to reconnect with my body and my feelings after having ignored them for many years. I understood God to be confirming my journey out of the marriage, into a more integrated spirituality, and into a more healing-centered ministry.

It has been six years since my first visit to Kirkridge and Columcile. I have returned many times. They are, for me, very sacred places, where I connect with God in a unique way. I have had other mystical experiences while visiting there in those six years. I expect there will be more. I have been out of my marriage for four years. I am still in parish ministry, mostly due to the financial need to support myself as I share custody of my children with their father. I haven't given up my dream of going back to school, having recently applied for a doctoral program in psychology. I have discovered some avenues for using healing more openly in my ministry, while waiting for the synchronicity of the universe to make my path clear for me, and struggling to trust that God will continue to be present in my life.

Christmas

In a number of workshops, I have asked people whether they have had one or more experiences that they would identify as an experience of God ... On average, eighty percent of the participants identify one or more and are eager to talk about them. They also frequently report that they had never before been asked that question in a church setting or given an opportunity to talk about it.

Marcus Borg

Marcus Borg, *The God We Never Knew* (San Francisco: HarperCollins, 1997), p. 53.

Visions Of The Nativity

Rochelle M. Pennington

When the angels had left them and gone into heaven, the shepherds said to one another, "Let us go now to Bethlehem and see this thing that has taken place, which the Lord has made known to us." (v. 15)

Visions. Conversation with God. Holy encounters with the Heavenly.

Until one evening during the Christmas season, 1990-something, I had never experienced any of these, but had always marveled at hearing stories of those who did, including the ancients of biblical scripture: Abraham, Jacob, Joseph, Moses, Jeremiah, Jonah.

"Incredible," I'd think, amazed that such divine dialogues could actually take place. My relationship with God, up until this point, was one continuous monologue: I talked, God listened ... I hoped.

But then it happened. And it happened like this ...

Our family had just returned from our annual pilgrimage to Holy Hill Cathedral in Wisconsin, a couple of hours from our home, to see the living nativity set up there beneath the night sky. Joseph, Mary, an angel, and kings took their place among the animals that included goats, sheep, a donkey, a llama, and even a camel. These are the ones who came, as we did, only once a year, only at Christmas.

There is "something" about this sanctuary atop the mount that draws visitors from around the world to pray, to worship, and to climb its towers that reach upward to touch infinity. And there are those who come for healing. Wheelchairs left behind, now empty, attest to the power of this place. Crutches and leg braces rest against the great wall, a visual affirmation of the lame who left walking. People pause and stare at the crutches, especially the little ones. Some murmur among themselves in wonder. Some are silent. What is there to say? Yes, there is something here that reaches out to you from somewhere else. One can sense it. And this was the backdrop for my vision.

We returned home that evening, following the nativity. We had eaten supper there in the old monastery cafe outside the cathedral: homemade chili and hot cocoa. We also stayed to hear the symphony concert, performed every Christmas in the great church with its marvelous acoustics, as we always do. The concert concluded with the traditional congregational singing of carols. If you've never experienced singing "Silent Night" and "Joy To The World" with a chorus of hundreds of other voices joined to your own, and hearing those voices accompanied by both a massive pipe organ and an entire orchestra, well, words fail to express what opens in your heart at such a moment. At least mine do.

It was particularly cold traveling home that evening. When we finally got to bed, with the heating blanket turned on high, sleep came readily. Then, sometime during my drowse, I heard a voice ask of me, "Who are you in Bethlehem?" I knew the voice was God's. I still wonder how I knew this, and I'm still unable to answer my own question.

My response was a less than brilliant, "Huh?"

Again came the question, "Who are you in Bethlehem?"

I was confused. How could God be asking me who I was in Bethlehem when *I wasn't even in Bethlehem*? If God is supposed to know everything, how could he not know rural Wisconsin is nowhere near the Middle East? God's question did not make any sense and I decided to tell him so. Perhaps this was not the brightest idea, but it was the only one I had at the time.

"I don't know what you're talking about," came my second and final contribution to the conversation. Then visions came, many of them: visions of shepherds and angels, of an innkeeper and a donkey, visions of a young woman named Mary, wise men, and a star.

"Look closely," God told me, indicating the innkeeper in Bethlehem. "I *still* stand at the door and knock," he said, "the door of every heart of humankind. Do you make room for me within you? Do you welcome me or instead say, 'I have no place for you;

my heart and my life are full'? Have you sent me to the barn of your heart, apart from you, out back, forgotten?"

"Look closely," God then pointed at a simple donkey, laboring to carry a woman, great with child, up hillsides. "Is this *you*?" he asked. "Are *yours* the humble efforts that serve in roles necessary, but so often taken for granted? Without the donkey, the Christ child would not have arrived in Bethlehem, nor could the church stand without the efforts of those who, in quiet humbleness, labor outside positions of attention. They build, they roof, they paint, they scrub bathrooms, they mow lawns and clear jungles in order that mission sites may be erected."

And then I saw Mary, kneeling before the angel Gabriel, bringing her the news that she had been chosen to give birth to the Messiah. I heard her respond, "Behold, I am the handmaid of the Lord. Let it be to me according to thy word."

"Is this *you*?" God asked, "Is *yours* a heart desiring acceptance of my will for your life? My will for your life is in my word. Does your spirit respond, 'Let it be to me'?"

Visions of other angels appeared, multitudes of them, their voices raised in praise from the skies above Bethlehem, "Glory to God in the highest!"

"Is this *you*?" God asked. "Do *your* lips proclaim my praise? Do *your* words example those of the Psalmist, 'I will bless the Lord at all times; his praise shall continually be in my mouth'?"

Then came the wise men, in search of the Christ child, asking directions to the one they had sought for two years: "Where is he that is born King of the Jews? For we have seen his star in the east and are come to worship him."

"Is this *you*?" God asked. "Are *you* determined to kneel before me and worship or do you, instead, have no time?"

"Look closely," God said, indicating shepherds hurrying to Bethlehem to find "a babe wrapped in swaddling cloths and lying in a manger" as told to them by the angels. After finding the Christ Child, "the shepherds then made known abroad all that had been made known unto them concerning the child. Everyone who heard the shepherds wondered at their telling."

"Is this *you*?" God asked. "Has the message of Jesus been made known unto *your* heart? Have you, like the shepherds of Bethlehem, taken this message to others? Do you go forth sharing with others the truths you have heard, and seen, and believed?"

Then the visions ended with one final face: that of King Herod, who wanted nothing more than the life and name of Christ silenced forever, as others still do.

But that did not happen, because shepherds of the message *kept coming* to tell all that had been made known unto them abroad, and donkeys *kept coming* to serve in a humble and necessary way, and angels *kept coming* to voice praise and glory unto the Lord, and innkeepers *kept coming* to make room in their hearts for the honored guest, and Marys *kept coming*, obedient to the will and word of God, and wise men *kept coming* to worship and kneel before the King of kings, and stars *kept coming* to shine the Light of the World to others.

"Look closely," God then told me of a star above Bethlehem, shining with brilliance. "Without words, the star's light proclaimed the message that Christ was among men and led travelers from distant lands to seek him.

"Is *this* you?" God asked. "Does the light of *your* faith radiate from within you? Are others led to seek the Light of the World by what they see, and not hear, from your life?"

I awoke and understood. Bethlehem's story is *our* story. When we look to Bethlehem, we look to ourselves.

As I crawled out of bed in search of pen and paper, my husband heard me and asked where I was going.

"God just spoke to me and I need to write this down," I told him.

He muttered something. I don't remember exactly what it was, but I think it went something like, "Huh? I don't know what you're talking about."

30

Kathy's Caterpillar

Diana Lampsa

*For the grace of God has appeared, bringing sal-
vation to all....* (v. 11)

On a recent August morning, I raced into the drive of a retreat
center, late for my morning appointment with Sr. Caroline, my spiritual director. The peace of the place seeped in, and I smiled at the
irony, wondering if I would race to my own funeral. Just then,
Kathy Bemmann shot into my mind, my good friend and colleague
who recently *had* raced to her own death.

It was Christmas Day in the year 2000, and I was joyfully nested
into my beautiful country lakeside home. For the first time in eleven
years of marriage, my husband Steve and I had decided we would
stay at home in peace rather than make the hectic drive several
hours north, and later south, to visit both our parents' homes. Bitter
cold had followed the weekend blizzard prior to this Monday holiday, making for icy and dangerous conditions. I had planned to
take the rest of the week as vacation from my psychiatric practice
and we would visit both our families during the week.

Relaxation and reflection seemed the order of the day, with
dinner planned at a friend's. I pulled out my guitar and started singing songs I had written in the late '70s, songs of searching for
purpose and meaning. It was refreshing to recall the feeling of one's
whole life lying ahead, wanting God's will to be done for myself. I
surveyed my current world and found myself restless, with too much
responsibility for the clinic I had founded. A key physician had left
early in the year leaving no one but Dr. Kathy Bemmann, my semi-
retired 69-year-old dynamo, and me, to pick up his large caseload.
The clinic was my dream, and its viability seemed threatened; I
wondered how my life had gotten so complicated.

Steve and I had settled in for an afternoon nap when the phone rang. It was Jamie Rambeau, M.D., who was on call from our local hospital. She said, "I hope this is a mistake, but I just got a call from someone saying he was a relative of Dr. Bemmann, and she was just killed." My heart pounded as I said, "Let's hope this is some kind of cruel hoax," and called the number she had given me. A man answered, saying he was Kathy Bemmann's brother-in-law, and gave me the news that Kathy had died in a car accident on the way to Christmas dinner at her sister's. "We thought we should call you first." I hung up and sat on the couch where I had made the call, and began to sob.

Somehow, I got through the next few hours, and about three hours after I got the call, went to my music room and began to write a song for Kathy. I can't recall exactly when her spirit began to visit me. Perhaps it was as I wrote her song, or the next day, as I met with her family at her home and found myself volunteered to call all the non-family names from her address book. She lived alone, widowed six years earlier. Being with all her things and her family was comforting. We wrote the obituary in the afternoon, with me giving thanks that I had not been traveling this holiday, so I could be there for the family and for staff and myself. Alone in my office, writing her obituary from voluminous notes and clippings from the family, I began to be aware of her presence, vibrant, radiant. Radiant! Reds and purples surrounded her face as she glowed with joy, her spirit a definite exclamation mark, as was her life. It was as though she was saying, "Have no fear, it's just GREAT here!" Unmistakable, vibrating purple/red/magenta joy surrounded her.

Talking with her niece, Janet, I recalled a recent dinner when Kathy had questioned me intently regarding my spiritual beliefs. I was getting ready to give a talk related to miracles at my church, which Kathy found fascinating. I found *this* fascinating, in view of her self-professed agnosticism. Kathy's life was one of profound faith in social activism, and in people's ability to change. She fought, in essence, for spiritual freedom, and was especially involved in women's health and domestic violence programs. In fact, at the time of her death, she was serving as Chair of the American Medical Women's Association Foundation, promoting research and education in women's health. Feminism was a passion for this pioneer; she certainly was not interested in a patriarchal, controlling god or his institutionalized dogma. Yet, she questioned me and stated she would come to the worship service!

She did not. Nevertheless, her niece said, "I think you put a chink in her agnostic armor." Perhaps I did, and maybe this helped her a little bit. At any rate, her spirit presence stayed with me, just over my left shoulder, beaming, gleeful. It was constant for about a week, and then intermittent. It always "looked" the same; mind you, I could not "see" her with my eyes, it was not a hallucination, but I could see her face and aura visually, in my mind's eye. I did not hear her voice; I could only feel her energy, which was consistent, intense, colorful, and joyful. It's hard to describe this kind of sight. Kathy was very strong willed and at times we clashed, but we truly loved each other. I think she came to let me know that she was okay, and more, to deliver the *amazing* news that the other side is wonderful. "Yes, Diana, there is life after death!"

Kathy always drove too fast, and her most recent gift to me may have been the thought I had as I drove into the retreat center, wondering if I would race to my own death. I picture her, late for Christmas dinner, flying over a knoll and finding herself over the center line, drifting out of the ruts in the ice made by earlier cars. I can see her yanking the steering wheel to correct her course, losing control on the ice, spinning around to hit a telephone pole with the driver's door. The forceful impact broke the telephone pole in two. The accident site is on the way to my retreat center; I stop and pray by the new telephone pole occasionally, when I am not in a rush!

Sitting on the summer lawn with Sr. Caroline, I told her of my experience, thinking of Kathy as I raced into the driveway. Suddenly, I noticed a bright yellow caterpillar inching its way across the lawn. We stooped to look. It was unusual, about three inches long with angora-type brilliant yellow fur, accented by pairs of black antennae down its back, and one final lone antenna as its tail. A workman came over and we all agreed we'd never seen one like it. He picked it up to save it, and Caroline said, "No, let it go." We continued our discourse, and I looked for the caterpillar a few minutes later, but he was gone. "See," she said emphatically, "rare and brilliant, he just inches his way, and he gets there. He has all the time he needs! Is he rushed? Pray for focus."

I am, I am. As I thank God for my many gifts, I ask for one more: *focus* on how to use my gifts most creatively, and *awareness* that I have all the time I need.

Three Days Of Meditation

Judy Von Bergen

I will greatly rejoice in the Lord, my whole being shall exult in my God; for he has clothed me with garments of salvation, he has covered me with the robe of righteousness, as a bridegroom decks himself with a garland, and as a bride adorns herself with her jewels. (v. 10)

Day One

We gathered in a large, pleasant lounge on Friday morning. Wide windows running the entire length of the room showed the sun shining on the green, rolling hills of Connecticut. Inside, by the back wall, tables were set up for participants to register alphabetically. Closer to the windows, simple tan chairs and couches were arranged into small "conversational" groupings. However, everyone was quiet. There were none of the quick pleasantries and nervous energies of newly forming groups. Even at the tables the people were whispering their way through registration.

After receiving their materials, everyone found a comfortable spot to look through the information. I chose a chair on the far side of the room. From this vantage point, I quietly examined the people arriving: a gray-haired woman in a gauzy blouse and white pants; a chubby thirtyish man with a tattooed bicep, wearing a sleeveless undershirt and shiny navy jogging pants that swished when he walked; a petite woman with curly brown hair and large eyes wearing a dark sweatsuit; another attractive, middle-aged woman in black leggings and a loose blue sweater. I estimated that ages ranged from low twenties to upper sixties; an unpretentious looking collection of five men and nine women.

When registration was completed, we were led to a small, windowless gymnasium. Along one wall there were tables set up with sound equipment. In the center was a ring of folding chairs in a perfect circle. We took our seats.

Before coming, we were to think and write about what was concerning us the most at this time in our lives. We officially began the afternoon by sharing this assignment, each taking a turn to speak. The rest of the group just listened.

I shared that I had experienced health problems in the past years. I had a breast removed due to cancer, and lived with frequent headaches. I hoped to improve my health through meditation. Other attendees had reasons as varied as their ages. The gauze blouse, a self-proclaimed earth mother, needed financial guidance; the blue sweater, an author, questioned what she wanted to do with her book; both a tattooed mechanic and a young female chiropractor wanted to be closer to God; a twenty-year-old au pair wondered what to do with her grief over losing her boyfriend. The dark sweatsuit, a wiry, petite fortyish woman with a low, wavy brown ponytail, identified herself as Alexandra. Her twin sister had died three years earlier, and she was still consumed with grief.

When Alexandra spoke, I could hear my children's voices.

I am the mother of triplets, two identical girls and a boy, now 25 years old. When they were younger, I had been concerned about them being too dependent on each other. As adults, they have proven to function well alone, with the blessing of still being exceptionally close. I keenly felt her pain, imagining my children having to go through that excruciating experience someday, knowing I was powerless to protect them from it.

Alexandra's large, brown eyes were downcast and her hands fidgeted in her lap as she told of her sister, Mary Janet. Despite living in different parts of the country with their own families, they had been extremely close, and spoke twice a day until Mary Janet's death. Alexandra had come to find a way to say good-bye.

After sharing, we were introduced to a goal-oriented meditation that evolved through music, movement, and emotional release. The room was darkened, the music loud. If you felt like crying, you cried: laughing, you laughed. If you wanted to move, you moved. No one paid attention to anyone else. We just focused on

36

what was in our own minds and hearts. This was interspersed with quiet meals and lessons.

At 10 p.m., we ended for the night and filed out in silence, tired, fully ready for a break. Most of us had rented rooms and headed our own ways. Alexandra lived close by, so she drove home.

Day Two

Our next time for sharing came Saturday morning, before we ventured into the work for the day.

I explained that I had become aware of how thoroughly I extinguished any emotions I deemed unpleasant. How could I learn to identify and release these feelings to benefit my mental and physical health? I had my work cut out for me.

Alexandra reported on the wonderful conversation she had with her husband when she got home. She had explained the meditation and the work she had started. He had held her as she cried, and encouraged her to "go for it." Her hands fluttered over her heart as she told us of the huge hole left there when her sister died.

Day two was a twelve-hour stretch of the same format, with no talking. The work was all internal dialogue, exhausting and gratifying. After the long day, we had one more chance to share. I eagerly awaited Alexandra's turn, and wasn't disappointed.

"I am an artist," she reported, "so it seemed logical when I envisioned myself painting during my meditation. It felt very real." Her wide eyes widened more. "I was working on a large picture, which turned out to be of God. In my painting, God was holding Mary Janet!" Her arms curved gently in front of her, leaving a space where I could envision her sister. "In the painting, Mary Janet was waving good-bye!" My eyes, along with Alexandra's, were filled with relief and damp with tears. "But there's more! I turned the painting over and was surprised to find another painting on the back!" With arched eyebrows, sitting straight in her chair, she swung her arms in a turning motion. "This one was of God, too, but he was holding me, here, back on earth."

We filed out of the room in quiet awe and headed toward our cars. We had worked hard and were ready for a break to absorb what we had learned. Our sharing had bonded us as a group, even though very few individual conversations had taken place.

Day Three

Sunday we gathered at 10 a.m. We would be finished with our workshop by 5 that evening, but never with the work. We followed the now familiar tasks that had made up the last two days. It wasn't until late that afternoon that we shared this day's, and the whole weekend's, meaning to us.

Blessings had occurred; prayers had been answered. The author overcame her fear of releasing her book for publication. The earth mother had gotten a call from a friend, offering her a car. I had felt God loving me, all of me: the angry me, the hateful me, the sad me, the generous me, the selfish me. I had learned that all of me was worthy of love. Would this help me stay healthy? I felt more mentally healthy already.

Angels had visited Alexandra. Angels had swirled down around her, and with them came all sorts of memories of times with her sister. She relived times they had been sad, times they had been naughty, and happy times. She remembered their dancing together as they grew up. "Attending a Catholic girls' school we were taught to dance, but since there weren't any boys, we always danced together. I always led," she explained with quiet pleasure, one arm around an invisible partner's waist, the other out to the side to slow dance. "I relived all those times we had together. It was incredible, but there's more! After all these wonderful memories, my sister came to me! There she was, with all her red hair." Alexandra's hands waved by her ears. "Mary Janet came to me as an angel, and she put her hand out to me and said, 'Let's dance, but this time *I* get to lead!'"

It took my breath away! I, who have seldom cried in years, found the tears and let them flow. What a gift to Alexandra; what a gift to all of us! I know now that my children, indeed any of us, need not utterly despair in the death of a person we love. We must say good-bye, but that does not mean that they need disappear completely from our lives.

The workshop was over. I had learned that it is possible for questions and prayers to be answered. Before we all headed back to our own homes and lives, I made sure that I spoke to Alexandra about the impact her experiences had on me. Her relaxed smile and parting words continue to delight me. "Now that Mary Janet is an angel, maybe she can be *your* guardian angel, too!" I know that anything is possible, so I am watching for that red hair. Knowing Alexandra's story has been a blessing to me. Maybe Mary Janet will be another!

Consolation

Lori Hetzel

With weeping they shall come, and with consola-
tions, I will lead them back.... (v. 9a)

My mother died on January 20, 2001. I am her only daughter,
and we were very close. She had lung cancer. A tumor broke one of
her ribs, causing much suffering. She came home from the hospital
for the last time on January 12, which was a Saturday. On Monday
she told me she had a dream in which she saw Jesus surrounded by
a white light. He talked to her, but she did not talk to him. I asked
her if she was afraid and she said no. I think she wasn't ready to
die, or that Jesus was preparing her. I thanked him for that vision.
At that time she was fully alert. One day later she was unconscious,
but I knew she could still hear all of us who were with her. Two
days before she died she was trying to talk. I brushed her hair,
bathed her, and put on her makeup. I gave her a kiss and told her I
would be right back. When I turned to leave, she said, "I love you."
Expecting her eyes to be open, I turned to her, only to find her eyes
closed. That was a very precious gift from her. Later that day, I
heard her calling out to her deceased brother, Rodwell. I believe,
perhaps, he was calling to her. Saturday we gathered by her bedside; I sang "Amazing Grace" and when I finished, she passed away.
Peacefully.

I cried every day for two months after that, in the morning, and
at noon on my way home for lunch. Every night I would sob myself to sleep. I would say out loud how much I missed her. I ached.
I prayed to God every night, "Lord, I know she is with you. I know
she is at peace. I only pray that I could feel her peace; then I know
I could get better. Amen."

On Saturday, March 31, sometime in the early morning hours,
I was in bed in our bedroom which is upstairs in the attic. There is

only one window, which faces west. We use blinds for our window treatment and they are closed at night. We get very little light up there. The sun rises in the east and would have come up behind the garage. Yet, as something very powerful completely woke me, I saw a radiant, yellow light (our walls and ceiling are painted off white). The light was everywhere. I was captivated by its beautiful color, and then I realized my mother's presence was in the room. It was so strong. She was everywhere in the light. I was laying on my back with my arms directly at my sides. I lay there with my eyes moving, looking side to side, up and down. I saw my husband sleeping next to me. I wanted to wake him, but couldn't move. Maybe I was afraid this extraordinary moment would go away. I was overwhelmed by the light and her being in my room. All of a sudden, I felt an inner peace flow through me. It started at my feet, and moved slowly throughout my body. It was such a deep, gratifying peace that words are inadequate to describe it. While this was happening, my eyes were gazing through the beautiful glowing light. When it left my body, I remember lying there with a contented smile on my face, knowing my mother was truly at peace. In my mind, I thanked God for this wonderful gift. And that is exactly what it was. Then I rolled over on my left side and went back to sleep.

I have not cried one teardrop since I had this fantastic experience. Yes, I miss my Mamma, but in a different way now. I felt her peace. I met with my pastor and told him of my experience. I said, "If this is what death feels like, then no one should ever be afraid." My pastor said that I had felt the spirit of God move through me, and I must say it was. I was once skeptical when people told about events like this. Now, I rejoice. I believe God wants us to tell others who are grieving that the spirit of God is alive and has not abandoned us. My faith in the Lord has tripled.

Epiphany

For mystical consciousness, it is essential that everything internal becomes external and be made visible. A dream wants to be told, the "inner light" wants to shine, the vision has to be shared.

Dorothy Soelle

Dorothy Soelle, *The Silent Cry: Mysticism And Resistance* (Minneapolis: Fortress Press, 2001), p. 13.

Revelation

Iris Ninis

*... for surely you have already heard of the Com-
mission of God's grace that was given me for you,
and how the mystery was made known to me by
revelation, as I wrote above in a few words, a reading of which will enable you to perceive my understanding of the mystery of Christ.* (vv. 2-4)

My mother was a musician in a dance band. Music and dancing were the fabric of my world. Vocal music is where my heart
has connected as an adult.

For several years, I searched for the musical experience that
would satisfy. After twenty years of singing with a church choir,
my heart ached for something more.

I joined a large, Christian community choir where the level of
music was challenging, and the director passionate. It was marvelous to sing amid those voices. One night of practice carried me
through the week. After a season of singing, the spring concert was
over. Aware of the upcoming commitment of both work and school,
I planned to "sit out" for a year, then return.

Just before that time arrived, the church I'd been affiliated with
for so long was in need of a director. Their former conductor had
moved out of state, and the position was still not filled. I volunteered to lead the choir in the interim. A talented young man was
soon hired, and I chose to stay for the remainder of the year while
he became acclimated.

In the meantime, my search for satisfying music continued. I
began arranging Sacred Sound workshops in the area, which explored the healing properties of sound. I decided to join a monthly
toning group. After only the second meeting, I sensed that it was
not right for me.

It was almost autumn again, and two years since I'd participated in the big Christian community choir. I auditioned and was
eager to return to a setting that fed my soul. However, much to my
disappointment, the director who had been such a joy to sing with
had recently retired. I would not continue there.

I longed for music that reflected all of humanity. I began visu-
alizing a World Music choir that performed pieces from various
cultural traditions. Thoughts ran through my mind about this often, and amazing things began to occur. Information was given to
me in dreams, such as, "Singing breaks down barriers — choirs
like this help create peace in the world," and so on. The new choir
director at church seemed, somehow, to be part of this, and together we were led through some incredible synchronistic events
around this idea.

I soon found myself singing in a choir he was directing at a
women's college where he'd been asked to perform multi-cultural
music. I didn't claim to understand what was happening. Trusting
God's spirit to lead, I was following what, for me, was not only an
opportunity to sing music that would finally satisfy my heart, but
also an opportunity to help support the idea of a World Music choir
which was providing a sense of spiritual purpose.

Clarity about my spiritual purpose was something I yearned
for. The younger of my two sons was preparing for marriage in
five months. I felt joy and gratitude for God's support and guidance during the parenting years that had now come to a close. In
the previous three years, my husband had barely been present, working two jobs to help cover my decrease in income due to a new
vocation.

Suddenly a major shift happened in the musical setting, as the
director announced his plan to move to the other side of the country. My "meaningful spiritual purpose," as I'd been viewing it, dis-
integrated. I was puzzled. Had this purpose never really existed?
Was my interpretation of the incredible events that led me to this
situation bogus? What a crock! I didn't understand it at all. In fact
I didn't understand *anything*. I was deeply humbled. Life was too
difficult to figure out, and I was done trying. My spiritual reality
fallen, I was disillusioned, and retreated to the arms of God.

My heart sank deeply, then my will collapsed. This surrender was one that reserved nothing: my heart, my will, my life. Your will be done, God. What it is, or even if it is, does not matter to me. I slept for a week. I was tired: tired of searching, tired of sorting, tired of fearing. I'd had enough. Life was way too confusing. I let it go-o-o-o ... *all of it.* My sons, now grown, were a blessing to me. The distance in my marriage had become very frustrating. I felt no purpose in my life, and the methods I'd counted on to interpret my world had proven grossly inadequate.

Not two weeks later, in the early morning hours, I felt my left leg jostling and fullness throughout my whole body. I felt a need to relieve myself — everywhere. In a state somewhere between awake and asleep, I got out of bed, took a pen, and sat at the kitchen table where there was paper. My hand began to write. As I wrote, the fullness in me began to diminish. I wrote and wrote, having no idea, nor caring, about what was being written, but that it was relieving the fullness in me. When I felt completely emptied, I set the pen down, went to bed, and slept.

In the morning, having vaguely remembered the experience, I picked up the paper and read these exact words:

> *Go within you to touch what is real.*
> *Feel it and sing it, share what is you.*
>
> *Release your heart to Me.*
> *I will make your life sing and satisfy your soul.*
>
> *It is with Me that your life will sing*
> *Your heart will sing with Me*
> *Your heart will sing through Me*
> *Your life will sing ... Me*
>
> *Go there and you will sing.*
> *If all is taken there, your heart will resonate a new life,*
>
> *It's all and it's everything — sing your soul.*
> *Go to the core, and from there, sing out.*

Release all that is not of it.
It will leave you with who you really are.
Who you are meant to be.

Two nights later, the experience happened again, and this prayer came to me:

Here in my belly is God's great light. A star, forever
*   radiant and bright.*
"Hold me within you, support and protect."
That star within me is everything, yes.
The sound of the ages is held within me.
As I go there and rest awhile, then do I see ...
It's all and it's everything that ever was —
A sound that supports — a sound that is love.
I go there and listen, and am ready to feel that sound in
*   me always ...*
forever — it's real.
"Resonate me, oh sound, holy light, shine in me al-
*   ways, pure and bright."*
"My center, my refuge, At One let us be."
"Home in you now ...
my heart's finally free."

I cried for the following six months for little to no reason: joy, gratitude, grief, love. Everything and anything prompted tears. For a year and a half writing has continued to come to me in the night: poetry, drawing, and dialogue. The "voice" of the dialogue, is that of mother, father, friend, lover, and teacher, depending on what my needs are at the time.

Through the writing, I am consistently directed to the light of God within.

Filled With The Spirit

Eileen Fink

He said to them, "Did you receive the Holy Spirit
when you became believers?" They replied, "No,
we have not even heard of the Holy Spirit." (v. 2)

I had been reading books on the baptism of the Holy Spirit, trying to figure out the controversy between the charismatic movement and mainline denominations. One evening, when home alone, I prayed a prayer to be filled with the Spirit and went to sleep. Sometime into the night, I felt myself being held to the chest of Jesus. The love I felt was like no other and I cannot express it. I awoke completely filled with God's love. I'll never be the same. I know that God loves me.

After my mother died, I just was not sure if she was saved or not. This really weighed on me, and I asked the Lord to let me know for sure that she was with him. One night, shortly after my prayer, I had one of those "real" dreams. I heard the front door open and looked around to see who was there. It was my mother. She was much younger and she had a "glow" about her. I awoke and thanked the Lord that I could now put my doubts aside. She was with him.

The Call Of God

Bill Dow

*Now the Lord came and stood there, calling as
before, "Samuel! Samuel!" and Samuel said,
"Speak for your servant is listening."* (v. 10)

On Ash Wednesday of 2000, I had a very powerful worship
experience. I was tired, cranky, and in a judgmental frame of mind.
I really didn't think that communion and being marked with ashes
should be administered at the same time. Ashes on Ash Wednesday, Communion on Maundy Thursday, that's the way it should
be. I was distancing myself from what was happening. I was just
about totally divorced from the service when the pastor asked me
and our Lay Leader to assist him with communion (darn)! We were
to assist him after we took communion at the first table. We were
using the intinction method, something we don't often do, and the
pastor had asked us to pass the loaf between us and break off a
piece of bread and eat it.

"Well, this is going to go well," I thought. Those who were
thinking ahead waited for the cup. Those who followed directions
got some more bread when they figured it out. I was really in a
wonderful state of mind by then! I got up and went behind the rail
and waited for the next table. The pastor handed me a loaf and one
of the cups, and I approached the rail to the first communicant. It
was Dick Bonney, a retired pastor in our congregation. I mumbled
something about the body and blood of Christ and offered the elements. As he communed, I began to feel the presence of the Holy
Spirit passing through me and the elements and on to him. As each
person took the communion elements, this energy flow intensi-
fied, and I found myself silently praying for each individual in a
way that I couldn't have planned or initiated.

After serving that table, I stood off by the side, waiting for the next table. That's when a voice said, "See? That's what it's like!" I don't remember much about serving the remaining tables. I was too confused (read shook up) to focus or channel any energy. I doubt that anyone noticed anything unusual during this whole time. I've been left to wonder if this is a call to higher ministry.

Letting Go Of All The Junk

Kay L. Bandle

*I mean, brothers and sisters, the appointed time
has grown short; from now on, let even those who
have wives be as though they had none, and those
who mourn as though they were not mourning, and
those who rejoice as though they were not rejoic-
ing, and those who buy as though they had no pos-
sessions, and those who deal with the world as
though they had no dealings with it. For the present
form of this world is passing away.* (vv. 29-31)

Since my fifteen-year-old son, Justin, died five years ago, I
have had numerous "happenings" that have been hard to explain,
other than that they are all gifts from God. And it is the dream that
I had exactly seven months after Justin's death that I will always
treasure. In the dream, Justin was glowing from the inside out. He
expressed three feelings to me: one, he was very, very happy; two,
he wanted me to meet his new friends, at which time I realized we
were surrounded by others who also glowed; and three, there was
a feeling of peace and love. Since, when Justin was alive, I was
always taking pictures, I naturally wanted to continue this tradition and began searching for a camera. I turned from the group,
who were arranging themselves for the picture, and scrambled to
find a camera. But, as I turned from the light of their presence, I
immediately saw darkness and piles of junk. As I dug through the
piles of stuff, I discovered one camera that didn't have film, another with a dirty lens, and a third that just wouldn't function. I
was totally frustrated. That's when Justin touched my arm and told
me I needed to work through *all the junk in my life*! I woke up
laughing and crying at the same time! I've never had a dream of

my son since, but it's amazing what comfort that one dream has given me over the years.

Kay dedicates her story to her son Justin Bobholz, 6-20-81 to 7-4-96.

Reasons To Live

Rebecca Henderleiter

*And the unclean spirit convulsed him and crying
with a loud voice, came out of him. They were all
amazed....* (vv. 26-27a)

Saturday, April 30, 1999, started out as a great day. I felt cheerful and full of energy, a welcome change from the gloom and depression I'd felt the week before. After catching up on some neglected housework, I went shopping for bridesmaids' dresses with my good friend who would soon be marrying my best guy friend. The excitement of the upcoming wedding had us giddy. All the planning and romance and remembering my own wedding nine years earlier made me miss my husband. He'd been putting in long hours on second shift and our weekends were usually so full that we barely had time for each other. I was really looking forward to getting home and spending some time with him.

It was so disappointing when I got home and he told me he'd already made plans to go watch a hockey game with one of his friends. I was enraged when he didn't come home at 10:00 like he'd promised. The next six hours I went through cycles of depression, worry, anger, and rage. When he finally came home, at 3:00 a.m., he said he and his friend had been having a long talk, and he announced he was leaving me. He could no longer tolerate my unpredictable moods and, although I'd been working on improving myself for a very long time, he felt that in some ways very little had changed.

We talked for about an hour, mostly me begging him not to leave me and saying I would get better. Then he went to bed, leaving me alone. I felt my spirit sucked out of my body like water from a drain suddenly unclogging. The darkness from the week before returned in full force. I believed that I was entirely hopeless and decided that everyone would be better off if I were dead.

I began my suicide plan by finding the sharpest knife in the house. I then checked the pulse lines on both my forearms and marked the major arteries with a pen. I decided which wrist to cut first, and that I would do this on my back deck, because I didn't want to leave a stain on my beige carpet. Then I began writing a suicide note, but it occurred to me that if I left a note, my husband would probably destroy it and no one would know the truth. So I decided to call my sponsor and leave my final message to the world with her. When I called, I got her answering machine and she didn't pick up. I felt it was because she didn't care. In reality, she wasn't in town. So I called my best guy friend, who got up to take my call at about 4:30 a.m.

I told him I was calling to say good-bye. He asked where I was going. Then I proceeded to tell him of my plan and asked him to make sure I got a proper funeral and that everyone knew it was my husband's fault that I died. He tried desperately to talk me out of it. He reminded me of all I had going for me: two wonderful kids, a nice car, a beautiful house, so many friends who truly loved me. But none of that mattered to me. I finally told the truth about how I felt inside. It seemed like every time I felt alive and happy, a dark cloud would pass over me and stay with me for two weeks. I was tired of living that way, and felt as if no one would ever love me because of it. He suggested that I might have something else wrong, some sort of mood disorder. This only strengthened my resolve to kill myself. It was bad enough being an addict. I certainly didn't want to be a mentally ill addict, a double social stigma! After about an hour and a half of this, he finally said, "Well, if that's what you really want to do, go for it. But you realize that your husband will probably find someone else who was just like you were before you got clean, and that woman will get to live in *your* house and raise *your* kids. If it were me, I'd get a lawyer and make his life a living hell!"

Oddly enough, by tapping into my rage, he saved my life. At 6:30 that morning, the sun began rising, the birds began singing, and I could smell the apple blossoms on my trees. The presence of life around me gave me the strength to hold on for one more day.

Later that morning, my very worried sponsor called me. I told her that I was no longer planning to kill myself and let her know the truth about what had been happening with my mood swings, something I'd kept secret for years. She agreed with my other friend, that it sounded like a mood disorder and that I should put in an emergency call to my therapist as soon as we hung up. She also asked me to write a list of reasons to live and afterward begin a Fourth Step to describe all I'd been hiding. (Step 4: We made a searching and fearless moral inventory of ourselves.) She would be moving out of state the following weekend, so we decided I would do my Fifth Step with her that coming Friday. (Step 5: We admitted to God, to ourselves, and to another human being the exact nature of our wrongs.)

I wrote furiously, and by Friday I had about twenty pages, double sided, of my moral inventory. The Fifth Step with my sponsor took about four hours. We cried, prayed, and even laughed together. When it was over I felt emotionally drained, but the weight of carrying around my secret was gone. It had been confirmed earlier that week that I did have a mood disorder, called bipolar type II, rapid cycling. With this confession and medical help, I was back on the road to recovery.

Step 6 is "We became entirely ready to have God remove all these defects of character." Mental illness is a medical condition, not a defect of character. Regardless, it didn't take me long to become entirely ready to ask God for help to rebuild my life.

Sunday, May 8, one week after my breakdown, was Mother's Day. It was also the day my husband decided to move out for awhile to get his head straight and make a decision about our marriage. That morning he went golfing. When he returned, he began packing while I went to a meeting. After I came home, he left. At first I felt incredibly alone. Then I remembered that God would always be with me.

I moved on to Step 7, "We humbly asked him to remove our shortcomings." I took that huge Fourth Step I had written out, and, without even looking at it, put it in a large coffee can. Then I dumped an almost full bottle of charcoal fluid on it, placed it on top of my grill, and set it on fire. I came into the house and lit the unity candle from my wedding and placed it behind me. I watched the huge flames from the coffee can through the patio door as I prayed and meditated. The small flame from the unity candle reflected in the glass. At times the flames from the can reached over four feet high. It burned for over forty minutes. The whole time, I asked God to reveal his will for me and to help me become whole again, regardless of what would happen to my marriage. When the flames finally went out, and the smoke cleared, I blew out the candle and went to bed.

The next morning, after I got the kids off to school, I went out to my deck to remove the coffee can and scatter the ashes from the burned paper. The coffee can was charred black inside and out. Everything in it had turned to white ash. Everything except one small scrap of slightly charred paper. Chills ran down my spine and my gut filled with fear. This was impossible! God was leaving me with something. Whatever it was, I didn't want it, and I ran back into the house. I paced circles in my living room as I prayed to remind God that I wanted him to take *all* of it away. Suddenly, I was filled with an incredible peace. I walked back outside and removed the scrap of paper from the can. It read: Reasons To Live:

My kids

My spiritual journey is not complete

It would be an insult to my God not to complete my life in his time

Awestruck, I put the paper back in the can. Tears streamed down my face as I felt the healing power of the Holy Spirit enter my heart. Just then, my sponsor's husband stopped by to see how I was doing. He was back in town to pick up another load of their things, and she'd asked him to check on me. When he saw my tears, he assumed I was upset and asked if he could do anything. I told him he'd just walked in on a miracle and took him to the back deck. I explained the ritual of the night before and asked him to read the surviving scrap of paper. After reading it, he collapsed to his knees and began sobbing, thanking God for allowing him to witness his work.

Others stopped by that day and were also shown the paper in the can. That evening, I scattered the ashes and disposed of the can. But that one little scrap of paper remains with me to this day, sheltered in a glass frame with an apple blossom. Whenever people tell me they don't believe in miracles, I show them mine and ask them if it could be anything but.

Thank you, God, for your wondrous works.

A Healing Presence

Lynette E. Metz

*That evening, at sundown, they brought to him all
who were sick or possessed with demons. And the
whole city was gathered around the door. And he
cured many who were sick with various diseases,
and cast out many demons.... (vv. 32-34a)*

During the late winter of 1992, the house was its usual hectic
scene while getting the family out the door for work and school.
My daughter, Jolene, was leaving for school when she poked her
head back into the kitchen to say that Dirty Snowball, one of the
three-week-old kittens, was out of his basket in our garage and
lying under my car.

Knowing that he was too young to be out on his own, I immediately went out to check on him. His little body was fairly stiff,
but as I cradled and turned him over in the palms of my hands, I
could see his tiny chin quivering. I wasn't sure if he was moving it,
or if it was from the movement of my hands. I ran into the house
with him and grabbed a hand towel to keep him warm. Sometime
in this sequence of events, I managed to call our veterinarian and
ask him a couple of questions. He told me to just give up and let
the kitten die. I couldn't do that.

Grabbing the hairdryer, I turned it on low and let it warm his
tiny little body while I prayed for guidance to know what to do.
Suddenly, I felt something over my left shoulder and turned to look.
I instinctively knew that it was Jesus, although I truthfully could
not have described him, even a moment later. As I looked at him, I
felt another presence over my right shoulder. I turned to look, and
immediately recognized a woman from Emmanuel United Methodist Church, Richfield, Wisconsin, who had died several years
before. Everyone took wild birds to Wilma "Grandma" Gerken

59

when they were wounded. She would care for them and release them back into the wild. Immediately, I knew what I had to do. I began abbreviated CPR on Dirty Snowball. With two fingers, I massaged where I guessed his heart was located, and blew short puffs of breath into his mouth from an inch or two away. After just a short time, he was back to life. Since I had college classes that morning myself, I called my neighbor and asked if she would be willing to watch the kitten for the day, and she could hear him meowing over the phone.

I believe that Jesus and Grandma Gerken came to give me the help I needed and to show that even the tiniest of God's creatures are being watched over and loved. None of us is ever alone.

God's Faithfulness

Edgar A. Evans

*O Lord my God, I cried to you for help, and you
have healed me. O Lord, you brought up my soul
from Sheol, restored me to life.* (vv. 2, 3)

As I look back over my relationship with God, two events,
which I believe were miracles, stand out that demonstrate the love
and faithfulness of God.

Both incidents happened about twenty years ago, when my
wife found a lump the size of an acorn in her breast. A mammo-
gram indicated that, on a scale of one to five, the result was about
a four and one-half, which would almost certainly be malignant.
The doctor explained to Marjorie that he probably would have to
perform a radical mastectomy. So, a date was set for her to enter
the hospital for a biopsy.

But, it turned out that she had a chest infection that had to be
cleared up before she could be given an anesthetic. So, for three
weeks, many relatives, friends, and people on prayer chains at several churches all interceded for her with prayer.

On the afternoon before the scheduled biopsy, I took Marjorie
to the hospital. The next morning, while shaving, I was extremely
nervous and felt as if I was coming apart. As I contemplated a
worst case scenario, my hands began to shake and I had to stop
shaving.

For three years I had taught the Gospel of John to my eighth
grade Sunday school class. I recalled John 14:27, "Peace I leave
with you; my peace I give to you. I do not give to you as the world
gives. Do not let your hearts be troubled, and do not let them be
afraid."

As those words popped into my mind, I said, "Father, where is
this peace that your Word promises? I have been teaching about it

for three years. Help me, Lord!" It was as if someone had turned on a switch, for immediately I was calm and peaceful, and even sang while driving to the hospital.

To me, that was the first miracle.

Before the doctor went into surgery, he said to me, "I will be out in about an hour if everything goes well. But I do have another surgeon ready to assist me if we find a malignancy."

An hour and a half later, my new-found peace was beginning to fray. When the doctor finally came out, he apologized for taking longer than he had told me. He explained that when he made the incision, the acorn-sized lump was no longer there. All that remained was some scar tissue. He sent a sample of it to the lab, and the result was benign. He couldn't believe it, so he sent two more samples to the lab, and they, too, were benign. He concluded by saying, "So your wife is fine, Mr. Evans."

Later, Marjorie asked the doctor if he thought what happened was a miracle. He said, "I've heard of such things. All I know is that you had a lump which is no longer there. There's no other way to account for it. So, yes, I guess I would say it was a miracle."

And, to me, that was the second miracle. How I praise the Lord for his faithfulness and his love!

Still Hope

John W. Doll

The Lord sustains them on their sickbed; in their
illness you heal all their infirmities. (v. 3)

My brother has a daughter who is as beautiful as any woman could ever hope to be. She married a man who is equally attractive, extremely intelligent, and an exceptional businessman. Most importantly, he is a dedicated Christian, and lives his life accordingly.

After the first few years of marriage, they had two equally beautiful daughters. Not too many years later, he owned a video shop, two Hagen-Daaz ice cream parlors, and a beautiful half-million dollar condominium. The family's life could not have been more perfect. With all this love and security, they had obviously been blessed beyond belief. They literally had everything.

Then one day, the husband, Wilson, reported feeling poorly. He had no specific complaint, but rather a general over-all sick feeling. Having had little or no illness in his life, he called my brother and asked if he had ever suffered such complete discomfort. When Ned heard the list of complaints, he realized he had never had so many problems. After more talk, and recognizing how badly Wilson was hurting, Ned finally suggested that he play it safe and have himself checked out at the nearest clinic.

Wilson went to a clinic in San Jose immediately. He was given the most complete physical he had ever had in his life and sent home with instructions to return the next day for the diagnosis. Wilson stopped at my brother's home on his way to have someone to talk to. Ned was very much concerned, but Wilson assured him that he had total trust in God, and whatever the final diagnosis was, he would accept it as God's will. Then he went home to wait.

When Wilson returned to the clinic the following day, he was directed immediately into the doctor's office. There were three doctors in conference there, going over x-rays, blood tests and other results of the exam. There were no smiles, handshaking, or small talk. Wilson was asked to take a seat. The silence seemed to last an hour, but it was really only a few moments before his original doctor finally spoke.

"Wilson, I'm afraid the diagnosis is not a pleasant one. I have the unfortunate responsibility to inform you that you have terminal cancer. Your whole body is infected. Your stomach, kidneys, and lungs are all clearly cancerous. I wish I could offer you some hope, but it would be unfair to your family, and most of all to yourself. This way, you will have at least several weeks to take care of your business and to make necessary arrangements."

Once again Wilson went to my brother. He calmly declared, "If God has decided to take me home early, I can live, and die, with his decision." There was no panic, but rather a deep sense of peace. He finally got up, shook Ned's hand, and went home. After the door closed, Ned dropped his head into his hands and cried until there were no tears left.

While Wilson made out his will, chose a cemetery and plot, and picked out flowers, my wife and I were in constant prayer for him and his family. Although he was in constant pain, and had to make trips to the clinic every other day for treatment, my brother reported on how peaceful Wilson continued to be.

About two weeks later, Ned called me again and asked if I had heard the news. Upset, I told him that I could guess, and not to give me any details. Ned said, "Now hold on, let me tell you the news!"

It seems the rest of the family had gone to sleep, but because of the continued pain, Wilson had stayed up reading a book. It was not hard to guess what the book was, but he was having a hard time concentrating on the text. Suddenly, he observed a ball of white light expanding at his feet. He became frightened, thinking perhaps this was another symptom of his condition. The light continued to grow, but as it reached his feet and ankles, he noticed a very specific warmth and comfort coming from it. The light continued rising on his body, and with it the warmth, releasing him from the pain and anxiety. By the time it had enveloped his body, he was totally free of pain. His body was relaxed and comfortable beyond belief. Wilson experienced a euphoria he had never known before in his life. The entire room was engulfed in the light that could only be described as being like a beautifully bright summer's day.

When the light began to diminish, Wilson noticed that the euphoria remained. He was pain-free, completely at peace, and even felt good enough to get up and do something. Suddenly he could feel his heart beat begin to accelerate as he wondered, "Did I die?" The only thing he could think to do to test this idea was to see if he could get up from the chair, get a drink of water, and go to bed. The euphoria did not dissipate as he crawled between cool white sheets and snuggled next to his wife, but he dreaded going to sleep for fear that, in the morning, the pain and reality of his diagnosis would return. However, in the midst of the joy and peace, he prayed his thanks and love to God.

Wilson woke in the morning and lay perfectly still as he surveyed his body's feelings. Not only was he still without pain, he was as happy as he had been the night before. And even more important, he was hungry! He wanted to pray his thanks forever, but he rose, dressed and ate so that he could greet a new day, not to die, but to live.

He waited a full day before calling the clinic, so that he could fully believe that it was not just a beautiful dream. The next day he went for an appointment, and, as on the day of gloom, was shown directly into the doctor's office. All three doctors were assembled, and did not appear to share the joy Wilson was feeling. They repeated all of the tests from his first physical, but had him wait for the results. Several hours later, Wilson entered the office again in their somber presence. His doctor once more assumed responsibility for breaking the news of their findings. "Wilson, we are not able to explain what has happened, but we have found no trace of the cancer in any of your organs or your blood. We can only say that you are cured and apparently healthy. I would say, God bless you, Wilson, but it would appear that he already has."

On his way home, Wilson stopped in at his office and worked for the rest of the day.

A Life Redeemed

Vickie Eckoldt

Bless the Lord, O my soul, and do not forget all his benefits — who forgives all your iniquity, who heals all your diseases, who redeems your life from the Pit, who crowns you with steadfast love and mercy, who satisfies you with good as long as you live so that your youth is renewed like the eagle's. (vv. 2-5)

At age 42, I was faced with two major surgeries within six weeks. I did not have the strength to recover properly and was faced with one setback after another. My condition continued to deteriorate for over a year. At 93 pounds, I was hospitalized again. I was told I would most likely be dead within two months, because my body just couldn't get stronger. Determined to prove them wrong, I went home and fought the best I could, only to become more exhausted.

One day, while lying in bed, totally drained, I felt I couldn't go on any more. I talked to God and said, "I just can't fight anymore, take me home and then I'll be at peace." Later I was startled by a white presence in the room. There was a beautiful image with his arms stretched out to me. I was being drawn closer and closer to him. I became frightened and realized what was happening. I then started to pull away, wanting to continue my fight here on earth. I prayed for the strength needed to get stronger. The image very slowly backed away and was gone.

It is now thirteen years later, and that image will always be with me as powerful as the day it happened. It changed my life forever.

Transfigured

Theonia Amenda

And he was transfigured before them, and his
clothes became dazzling white, such as no one on
earth could bleach them. (vv. 2b-3)

We were standing in a circle in an open, mowed field on a mini-farm outside Nashville one summer day, worshiping God and saying good-bye to our retreat leader, who had just been elected to be a Bishop. As we held hands while someone prayed for him, I found I could not keep my eyes closed. I wanted to gaze at this gentle, deeply spiritual man, for whom I had great admiration and respect. He was standing across the circle from me in his blue jeans and red checked shirt. My heart was sending him a great deal of love and God's energy as I listened to the words of the prayer.

All of a sudden, a strong golden-white light appeared at his feet, on his right side, traveled up his body to his head, where it swirled around and around, then traveled down his left side. He was aglow with light, which was reflected off the persons on either side of him. I kept blinking my eyes, trying to clear them, to see if this light was being caused by something in my eyes, but it was not.

I felt as if time was standing still as I listened to the drone of a voice continuing to pray, heard a horse neighing down in the barn, and saw a dog walking around in the middle of the circle. I continued to watch the illumination of a man as about fifty of us sent out our love and support, asking for God's blessings and power to be poured out upon him.

After the prayer had been lifted up, a deep, deep silence fell over us. It was a silence that was almost audible. I wonder if it was like what the scriptures said Elijah experienced outside the cave as he was listening for God. One version of that scripture said that Elijah heard God "in the sound of sheer silence."

That describes the deep silence at that moment in our circle of love. Eventually that silence was broken as our song leader lifted her voice, inviting us to join her in a closing hymn. I heard others say later that they wished the silence had not been broken so soon, but no one spoke of what I saw.

I kept that experience within me until the next time I saw the Bishop, which was months later. I dared share with him what I had seen that day in that mowed field outside Nashville as we said good-bye to him. His response was acceptance, wondering if that accounted for his high level of energy as he began his new task, which he had not sought, but had answered as a call from God.

Lent

Assuredly, Western Christianity has a rich mystical tradition. But how often were mystics ignored or marginalized or persecuted by an establishment that put its emphasis on words and letters, on doctrines and dogmas, on the strict observance of church law? ... The tragedy of Western Christianity is that there were, and are, so few mystics in the establishment.

William Johnston

William Johnston, *Arise My Love: Mysticism For A New Era* (Maryknoll: Orbis Books, 2000), p. 138.

Ronny's Gift

Rebecca Henderleiter

Create in me a clean heart, O God, and put a new and right spirit within me. Do not cast me away from your presence, and do not take your holy spirit from me. Restore to me the joy of your salvation, and sustain in me a willing spirit. Then I will teach transgressors your ways, and sinners will return to you. (vv. 10-13)

In recovery circles, many tight-knit relationships are formed. Fellow recovering addicts or alcoholics form bonds that transcend those of blood relatives, making us "family in spirit."

One of my closest bonds was with my "big brother" William. We had a brother/sister relationship that we were unable to obtain with our blood relatives. Our friendship began shortly after he completed treatment and we began doing service work together. We were always there for each other, sharing the growing pains and joy of freedom from active addiction.

In the spring of 2000, I was devastated when William chose to go back to drinking, one week before his nine-year recovery anniversary. Many of us were hurt and dismayed over his relapse and tried everything to get him back. But I believe it was hardest on me, because I was babysitting his son at the time and I saw him almost daily. I watched the light of the Spirit fade from his eyes as he became just another statistic.

He would often bring me different kinds of recovery memorabilia and ask me to pass it on to someone who could use it or would have special appreciation for it. Upon receiving these items, I'd tuck them away and save them for the day he was ready to come back to recovery.

William worked in a salvage yard. One day, he brought me a twenty-year-old treatment center graduation medallion. It had belonged to Ronny, a recovering alcoholic who had died the previous month. Ronny's van was scrapped after his death, and William had found the medallion in it. William said he would have kept it for himself, but he hadn't spoken to Ronny in years and thought it should go to someone he was close to before his death. Although I had known Ronny since I began my recovery, we were not very close. The only memories I had of him were his joyful smile and warm hugs. I knew the medal was not meant for me, so I prayed and asked God and Ronny to let me know where it belonged. I felt the answer deep in my gut, "It belongs to William. Save it for William."

About nineteen months later, I left my husband. I moved in with friends who live a half hour away from my house. My husband allowed me to come and go as I pleased, but I avoided moving anything from the house while my children were at home. This left me with few people available to help me. My friend Bill had a day off and told me he'd help me move a couple of heavy objects that I'd been putting off. We loaded my truck and reminisced about how things were when we were new to recovery.

He shared a story about Ronny. When Bill was in treatment, he was acting completely disrespectful in a meeting while Ronny was sharing. Without missing a beat, Ronny said, "Hey, kid, if you want to play games I think they've got Monopoly upstairs. I'm here to save my life, and if you're interested in saving yours, you'll shut up and listen!"

Bill was humiliated, but from that point forward he was never disrespectful in a meeting again. Meanwhile, Ronny took Bill under his wing. He ended up becoming a surrogate father for Bill, helping him to heal from the abuse he endured from his real father. Ronny also had a knack for giving Bill gifts that were just what he needed at the time. Ronny's death was very hard on him. He shed tears while sharing his stories of Ronny on our way back into town.

I remembered the medallion and wondered if I should give it to Bill. Again, I prayed and asked God and Ronny for guidance. The answer deep in my gut was, "You are supposed to give it to

72

William." I questioned this, as it seemed that Bill would be the right choice. The answer was, "Don't you realize that Bill is short for William?"

I immediately called Bill and told him I needed to come over and talk to him as soon as possible. When he asked why, I told him I needed to talk to him about William. I polished up the old medallion and headed over.

My story began with how much I missed my "brother" William, and that I could relate to his feeling of losing Ronny, because, in a way, William had died in spirit. Then I told him about William giving me things, and that I always held on to them in hopes that he would return to us. "But there was one thing that's not for him; it's for you. And it's not from me; it's from Ronny," I said, placing the medallion in his hand.

He asked how I got it. My reply was, "I guess Ronny really wanted you to have it, so he told me to give it to William. It just took me a while to figure out which William he was talking about."

We both sat there sobbing. Bill felt a strong presence of God's love. I had a physical feeling of an angel wrapping its wings around me. That angel was Ronny.

I still think of William often. Every day I pray for him. Sometimes I ask Ronny to wrap his wings around William and bring him back to our family.

The names of Rebecca's friends have been changed in this account to protect their identities.

A Dog With Soul

John Zingaro

*Then God said to Noah and to his sons with him,
"As for me, I am establishing my covenant with
you and your descendants after you, and with every living creature that is with you, the birds, the
domestic animals, and every animal of the earth
with you...." (vv. 8-10)*

When I lived in Tanzania, one day I was in the parking lot of a
game park. People were milling around. In the background, watching our every move, were baboons waiting for any scrap of food to
be dropped.

One baboon apparently got tired of waiting. He scrambled on
all fours across the parking lot and leaped onto the back of a Land
Rover. Nobody was in the vehicle, the people having gone into the
park office. With one hand, the baboon *opened* the rear door, got
into the car, came back out a moment later with a box of cookies,
and sprinted for the trees. I was impressed.

When we realize there are some animals who exhibit intelligence and other human-like behavior, the question naturally arises:
Does an animal have a soul?

What *is* a soul?

A British officer in the Battle of Lake Erie, in 1812, lost an
arm and a leg. He wrote to his fiancee back in England, telling her
what he looked like and offering to release her from the engage-
ment. She wrote back that so long as there was enough of him to
contain a soul, they would marry.

A soul is that something about a person which is still that person no matter what else changes. In the Bible, the Hebrew and
Greek words for "soul" are from the words meaning "to breathe,"
as though the soul is the very breath of life in a person. A soul also

has a relationship with God, as in the creation story, where we are made in the image of God.

So, does an *animal* have a soul? If not a soul, there may at least be something *spiritual*. It is arrogant to think that God works *only* through human beings.

Consider a story from the life of nineteenth century naturalist John Muir. Born in Scotland, Muir grew up in Wisconsin, near Portage. He explored Alaska with a party of American Indians, and a member of the party owned a short, black and white dog. One evening, Muir went off on his own, climbing over a glacier, and the dog trailed after him. After hours of hiking, they came to a wide crevice. As night was falling, rather than spend hours going around the gaping hole, Muir cut steps into the sheer side of the glacier wall and descended to a slender ice bridge, leading the dog step-by-step. A slip would have sent both to their deaths.

At one point, the ice bridge was only four inches across. When they finally had gingerly crossed the bridge and climbed back to the top of the glacier, Muir reported (and his biographer Linnie Marsh Wolfe wrote) that the dog was *jubilant*.

The dog, named Stickeen, gave out "a gush of canine hallelu-jahs!" Delivered from peril, Stickeen literally howled with glee. Muir said, "... he shrieked and yelled as if saying, 'Saved! Saved! Saved!' "

This is more than the behavior of instinct!

Days later, when Muir would be leaving the others in the party, he sat with the brave little dog on a wharf, saying farewell. When Stickeen was taken by his owner, "crying and struggling" into the canoe, "John Muir stood on the wharf, gazing after the small dark figure of the dog leaning over the stern of the [canoe] moaning for the friend he would never see again."

Twenty years later, in 1899, Muir was on a ship sailing past that same shoreline. He was sailing with a party of sportsmen and explorers returning from the Arctic Circle. While they were throw-ing a party below deck, Muir quietly went up to the railing so he could look at the wharf where he had said farewell to the dog, Stickeen.

"There (he paid) silent tribute to the brave little mongrel dog who, over there on the back of a dim white glacier, had followed him across the icy abyss."[1]

To think that a person could be so deeply touched by the company of an animal, who would dare say that the spirit of God is *not* involved?

---

1. Linnie Marsh Wolfe, *The Life of John Muir, Son of the Wilderness* (Madison: University of Wisconsin Press, 1945), pp. 218, 219, 287.

No One Is Lost

Keith R. Eytcheson, Sr.

*For he did not despise or abhor the affliction of
the afflicted; he did not hide his face from me, but
heard when I cried to him.* (v. 24)

A few years ago, one of my nephews went through an emotional break-up with a girlfriend. She began dating a friend of his, and he was very upset. He confronted her late one night, and after a long, loud argument, he shot himself. This young man's death prostrated his family. It was a very tragic time for all of us.

Some days later, my wife, children, and I were driving across town. As I pulled through an intersection, my nephew suddenly appeared in front of the car, seemingly suspended in midair. I stared in shock as he said to me, "Tell them I'm okay." Then he disappeared.

I drove ahead to the nearest parking space, pulled the car over, and began to weep. My wife, taken by surprise, asked, "Keith, what's wrong?" I told them what I had seen and heard. They had seen nothing.

But my daughter had been a close friend of my nephew. She had gone shopping with him in Milwaukee the night before his death. I was surprised when she asked, "Dad, what was he wearing?" I described the shirt and Levis he had on as he appeared there in midair before me.

"That was a new shirt," she said. "I helped him pick it out the night before he died." Of course, I had never seen the shirt.

When I told his family about my strange vision, I included my daughter's information about the shirt. His father said it was the shirt he was wearing when he killed himself.

"He said he was okay," his father repeated. They were both comforted.

Waiting For God

John Sumwalt

The heavens are telling the glory of God: and the
firmament proclaims his handiwork. (v. 1)

I begin my prayer time some mornings with the following
meditation. I go back to a sacred spot from childhood, on the bank
of the creek across the road from the barn on the farm in Richland
County, where I grew up. I pass an old abandoned boat which sits
in the weeds along the way. The creek is different every day. Sometimes the water is low, the ripples below the deep hole barely audible as they trickle over the rocks. Other days, after a storm, the
banks are full and I watch in awe as the water rushes around the
bend carrying debris from burst beaver dams and farmers' fences.
On bright, sunny days, I lay on the bank and warm myself as I
ponder the shapes of the clouds floating above. Most days I sit on
the bank and stare into the water. There are trout, suckers, horned
daze, chubs, minnows, and a great snapping turtle who has lived
in the hole for years and years. Once in a while, a mink or a musk-
rat swims into view. In the evenings the frogs sing and fireflies
light up the dark. Deer and raccoon come to drink and socialize
with their kind. A lynx calls out from a tree somewhere below the
bluff about a quarter mile downstream. His plaintive cry sounds
almost like the wail of a newborn child. Mosquitoes buzz around
my ears as I listen and watch. On spring days there are pollywogs
and tadpoles playing in the shallows with crayfish and waterspiders.
Dragonflies hover over the water and crows caw from the tops of
the tall cottonwoods. A kingfisher dives from a dead limb and
clutches a squirming fish in his beak. Goldfinches swoop in and
out of the willows that line the banks. I disturb the Great Blue
Heron as he feeds his way upstream. He flies abruptly straight out
over the water following the curve of the winding creekbed until

he disappears from view. I follow down a narrow path into the cool heart of the glen to the spot where my brothers and I once built a hut with willow branches. I rebuild the hut around me and wait for the primordial one....

My Labyrinth Prayer

Ann Watson Peterson

Then they cried to the Lord in their trouble, and
he saved them from their distress.... (v. 19)

On a cold, snowy evening, I climbed the stairs of Calvary Presbyterian Church to walk the Labyrinth with members of my church. I had participated in Labyrinth walks on a number of occasions, and was excited about introducing this ancient spiritual practice to them. I had initiated this gathering, but as I walked up the slippery stairs and into the church, I just wanted to go home.

I greeted them, explained the history of the Labyrinth, what to expect once they entered the sanctuary, and that they were to remain silent throughout their walk. Then I was on my own. I wrestled with my own need to walk. I was physically and emotionally exhausted. My mind was swimming with so many life choices that I felt I couldn't possibly concentrate on communing with God in this sacred space. But somehow I found myself standing stocking-footed on the edge of the giant circular path, daring God to meet me there. My final gesture was to dump the weight of everything I was carrying onto God. "Here you go," I said. "You deal with this: I can't anymore." Then I stepped onto the Labyrinth.

My first few steps were difficult. I had trouble getting my bearings. As with other walks I had taken, I found I was being critical of whether I was "doing it right." But as I walked, I began to feel more centered and my breathing righted itself. I noticed that my feet had slowed their frantic pace and my hands became unclenched and hung loosely at my sides. I was ever more aware of my breathing — in, out, in, out. As the air filled my lungs, I sensed a peacefulness I had not expected. In my awareness, I felt something that was new and unsettling. I felt as if I was being encouraged by some unknown "something" to name my troubles. I wondered who was speaking to me in such an unfamiliar way. And then a feeling came to me, or better, a voice: a knowing. It came from beyond *and* deep within me. I knew, then, that it was God speaking to me through what I can only describe as a still, small voice. In a silent plea, I said, "I am so scared, so confused. I don't know what to do." I "heard" God respond, "Yes, you do ... you know exactly what to do. You just don't want to do it."

I continued to walk. "But I'm afraid," I said. God responded yet again, "You are courageous, Ann. You have been through more difficult things than this." I thought for a moment, and then said to the "knowing" inside of me, "But I don't think I can do this all by myself." And God said, "You don't have to worry, I'm here with you. You are never alone." A peace settled over me almost instantly. All the stress I felt during the day seemed to vanish. I was surprised to find that all through the conversation I had been walking, but was unaware of my own footsteps. I was in my body, but outside of it. My encounter with God was very real and tangible to me. I looked up to see that I had made it to the center of the Labyrinth, where spiritual travelers rest in God before beginning the journey back out again. I had walked to the very heart of the sacred path, the very heart of God. I sat silently in the center in a posture of utter receptivity and gratitude. I just rested with God, and in God. As bliss-filled as I was, I became aware that my journey was not yet over. I had been called to action; I had some business to attend to. I stood and began my walk back out. My troubled mind and heart were now inexplicably freer and lighter. But I found myself trying to make sense of what had just happened. Had I really just "talked" to God? Did God really "talk" to me? Within the last remnants of the profound interchange, God "spoke" once again. "Don't try so hard. Just trust and believe." I almost laughed out loud. I stepped off the Labyrinth confident of what I needed to do, knowing that God would companion me along the way. And no matter what the outcome, I was going to do God's bidding.

Then A Voice Came

Loxley Ann Schlosser

Then a voice came from heaven, "I have glorified
[my name], and I will glorify it again." The crowd
standing there heard it and said that it was thun-
der. Others said, "An angel has spoken to him."
Jesus answered, "This voice has come for your
sake, not for mine." (vv. 28b-30)

Jim and I were married on September 8, 1979. We chose to be married in the Lutheran church where my deceased husband and I had been members. After we were married, Jim continued to attend services at the Catholic church where he was an active member, participating in the choirs as well as reading scriptures during the mass.

After several months, I chose to meet with a priest and began the process of studying in preparation to become a member of the Catholic church, so that we could worship together as a family. I have two daughters from my first marriage. At the time Jim and I married, my girls, Kimberly and Kristine, were ages six and four, respectively.

We attended mass every Sunday, enrolled our girls in Catholic school, and became a very happy family. We enjoyed attending church and school activities. Both of us sang in the choirs and taught religion on Wednesday evenings to children from our parish who attended public schools. Jim and I were re-married in the Catholic church in 1980, and I received the sacraments as required. I felt very good about having become a Catholic, although I never understood anything about church dogma and just couldn't accept the need of confession to a priest.

In 1986, Jim began attending private home Bible study. The study group consisted of people from different denominations:

Catholic, Lutheran, Baptist, Methodist, and Assembly of God, all from local churches. After just a few weeks, Jim was acting very differently. He began talking about Jesus in an intimate way, as if he and Jesus were close friends. He said things that I couldn't quite grasp, insisting that he had been born again and that Christ was alive within him. He was so excited, about the Lord and reading the Bible every spare second, that he was driving me crazy.

Jim began attending church on Sunday mornings and Sunday and Wednesday evenings at the Assembly of God church, always carrying his Bible with him and being excited about what the minister was teaching. He wanted me to go to the Assembly of God church with him, and he said all the people were praying for me. Jim said that I had to be born again. He was always reading his Bible and constantly "preaching" to me. I was still a very active member of the Catholic church, and frankly, I was not interested in going to a church where people would raise their hands in church and babble. I felt confused, angry, and determined not to go with him.

Jim became more and more involved with his new church. At Christmas they presented a musical drama, "The Gospel According to Scrooge," and Jim was in the play. On Saturday night he pleaded with me to go with him to see this production. I got very angry and said, "No!" After he left for the church, I mixed a batch of cookies to bake for the girls. I put the tray of cookies in the oven and started thinking about Jim. Then the timer went off, indicating that the cookies were done. I opened the oven door, and without any hot pads, I reached into the oven and lifted the hot tray of cookies with my bare hands. Needless to say, they were severely burned. As I ran cold water over the burns, a voice spoke to me as clearly as if someone was standing next to me, "Loxley, you belong in church with your husband." The Lord was speaking to me ... and my hands immediately stopped hurting!

When Jim came home, I showed him my hands. There were raised red welts, like blisters, on both of them. I told Jim my hands did not hurt, and that the Lord had spoken to me as clearly as I was speaking to him.

Sunday morning, when I awoke, there was no trace whatsoever of any burn marks on my hands. If Jim had not been a witness

83

to this event, I would have thought I had dreamt it. That evening, I went to the play at church and felt closer to God than at any other time in my life. Following this, I began to attend church and Bible study with Jim on a regular basis. I was baptized and now have a very personal relationship with God.

Holy Week
And Easter

At the height of his illness in December 1954, Pope Pius XII had a vision of Christ in which the savior spoke to him in "his own true voice." The Vatican kept Pope Pius' revelation secret for nearly a year, then through the "affectionate indiscretion" of one of the Holy Father's close friends, the picture magazine *Oggi* broke the story in its November 19, 1955 issue.

Brad Steiger

Brad Steiger, *Revelation: The Divine Fire* (Englewood Cliffs: Prentice Hall, Inc., 1973), p. 14.

A Plea For Help

Christal Bindrich

Let your face shine upon your servant; save me in
your steadfast love. (v. 16)

My mother died of breast cancer in 1976. I was 25 years old at the time, and the youngest of her three children. Soon after she died, she would come and talk to me in my dreams. I would feel her presence and would be comforted, knowing that she lived on in heaven. She would also come to one of my brothers in his dreams.

About two years after she died, she appeared in a dream to three people in my family on the same night. The dream was similar for all of us. She simply wanted to tell us that it was time for her to move on, that we didn't need her comfort, that we were all okay now. I guess she felt our hardest grieving was over. She said good-bye and promised that she would always be near when we needed her.

Even though I thought of her almost daily, she didn't appear in my dreams for many years. Then, in my third year of seminary education, she reappeared when I asked for her. It was during a particularly difficult time for me, where I was having trouble sleeping for weeks on end. I needed the comfort that only a mother can give, and so I prayed to God that she might come and hold me during the night, so that I could get uninterrupted sleep.

With that prayer on my lips, I fell asleep. Soon, I felt the comfort of my mother's arms wrapped around me, holding me as I slept. I didn't wake once that night, nor did I have one of the intense dreams that had been wearing me down. In the morning, I awoke feeling renewed and hopeful. I knew that my mother, though long departed from this physical world, was still watching over me and would always be there when I needed her.

Blessed At The Core

Manda R. Stack

I give you a new commandment, that you love one another. Just as I have loved you, you should love one another. By this everyone will know that you are my disciples.... (vv. 34, 35)

"Why didn't my parents have me baptized when I was an infant, like most other people in my church?" I wondered this as I carefully worked at my hair with the curling iron. It was Thursday, April 19, 1984. I was fourteen years old, and I was nervous and self-conscious about the evening ahead. At the same time, I was trying to be in a reflective state of mind, aware of the importance of the evening. It was Maundy Thursday, the very first time our Confirmation class would take communion, but more importantly, it was the day of my baptism at the United Church of Christ in Delevan, Wisconsin.

Maundy Thursday, we had learned in Confirmation, was a day to commemorate the Last Supper of Jesus before he was put to death on Good Friday. It was tradition in our church for eighth grade Confirmands to take their first communion together on this night. We would be confirmed together the next month. I had not been baptized as an infant, as had most of my peers. Baptism was an important part of becoming a confirmed member of the church.

I was rather casual and sometimes flippant about my faith as I sought to fit in with the group of about eight Confirmands. I walked the line between not wanting to appear too religious and also seriously struggling with some big questions of faith.

As a young teenager, I was not particularly looking forward to going up in front of everyone at church by myself and being baptized. My parents would be there. My friends would be there. But there was also a warm glow inside of me, and I looked forward to this sacred event. Baptism was supposed to be a marking by the Holy Spirit. I was curious to see what it was like on the receiving end.

I waited in the living room for my ride. The Confirmands had to be there early, and my parents would come later. My friend Kristina rode up our driveway in the passenger side of the car, driven by her older brother, Eric. I got into the back seat with the radio booming around me. We drove the short distance to the church, and the music blared.

At the church it was quieter. We were given last minute instructions. Our eighth grade Confirmation class sat together in the front two pews on the right side of the sanctuary during the service. We were all a bit antsy. About halfway through the service, before communion, Reverend Rigert called me over to the baptismal font. I went and stood to the side of the church, under the large stained glass window, by the font. He said some words about the Holy Spirit coming down like a dove, and that we remember Jesus' baptism: that this was a blessing and a renewal. The sanctuary was quiet. He asked my parents some questions about supporting me in faith. They said, "We do." He asked me some questions about my readiness. I said, "I am."

He told me to kneel down next to the font. I knelt and bowed my head. The self-consciousness had left me. He cupped his hand and brought some water out of the bowl and over my head, touching my head three times. "In the name of the Father, the Son, and the Holy Spirit. Amen." Water rolled down my hair and face, onto my shoulders. It felt cool. It felt electric. It felt like a mark of God. After a prayer, I was back on my feet. I walked across the front of the sanctuary to my place in the pew with the other Confirmands. I sat down among them a different person.

I felt open and hollow inside: airy, like the top of my head was open and the Holy Spirit was flying in and out of me, and around me. It felt white and soft, like clouds. I wondered if others could see anything wispy and white hovering by my head. The Holy Spirit was touching me and moving through me. And I felt blessed. Renewed. Healed. Loved.

During communion, we knelt around a table in the front for the bread and the grape juice. We were a bit awkward, trying to do things right and not spill. Tim stuck his tongue deep into the little cup and there was a noise that caused some stifled giggles around our table. But I still felt full of light and peace, and it seemed that my fellow Confirmands glowed with a new brightness.

I will never forget that feeling of the top of my head swirling with holy, white light, as if God went down into me and blessed me at the core. What a privilege it was to be old enough to consciously receive my baptism and remember it always.

I am now an ordained minister in the United Church of Christ. Although I did not consider being a minister until I was in early adulthood, a seed was planted years ago for my call to ordained ministry. When I baptize infants, and sometimes older children or adults, I am ever mindful of the Spirit of God that is present during the sacrament. Baptism is a visible sign of an invisible event. What an honor it is now for me to help facilitate the touch of the Holy Spirit onto God's children. Thanks be to God.

The Power Of The Cross

Wendy Wosoba

"This is the covenant that I will make with them
after those days, says the Lord: I will put my laws
in their hearts, and I will write them on their
minds," he also adds, "I will remember their sins
and their lawless deeds no more." (vv. 16-17)

As a young wife and mother and teacher, I was striving to be perfect. Every morning I would start the day with the goal of perfection. I would be the perfect wife, mother, teacher, friend. I went to bed each night as a failure. I was exhausted and, I suspect, I was on the verge of depression. Then, one Sunday morning as I entered my pew at North Presbyterian Church in Milwaukee, my whole life changed. For a brief moment, I was on the cross, hanging in front of the sanctuary.

To this day, thirty years later, I can't explain it. I don't remember any words. It was simply presence, Spirit. I knew how deeply I was loved and cared for. I didn't have to be perfect. I didn't have to prove my worthiness. The feeling of freedom was overwhelming. I don't know why I was blessed in such a way. I am forever thankful. I feel certain it saved my life.

For years I never shared this with anyone, but it was always with me. It changed the way I relate to others. Now every time I tell this story, or write about it, I am amazed at the power of the experience. It has sustained me all of these years and made my life a real joy and blessing, and yet it was so simple.

My Dad, Marlie

Patricia Gallagher Marchant

*For I handed on to you as of first importance what
I in turn had received: that Christ died for our
sins in accordance with the scriptures, and that he
was buried, and that he was raised on the third
day in accordance with the scripture, and that he
appeared to Cephas, then to the twelve. Then he
appeared to more than five hundred brothers and
sisters at one time, most of whom are still alive,
though some have died.* (vv. 3-6)

My dad died four years ago, and I am deeply at peace knowing
he is free of the inner torment he endured in his adult life.

Dad decided to undergo an elective surgery to open his carotid
arteries. They do one side at at time, and his first procedure went
well. He recovered, felt better, and decided to have the other side
done right away. While in the recovery room after the second surgery, he had a stroke. The next six weeks, I witnessed my father
preparing to let go, slowly going, and, on July 30, 1997, at 2:30
a.m., passing on. I had felt restless that day, awoke at the time of
his passing, and received a phone call from my Mom at 3:00 a.m.
confirming that he had died. Dad was free. We were stunned, sad,
and relieved.

Dad came to me a number of times within days and weeks of
his passing. The morning after his death, I was with Mom when I
saw Dad, a shadowy figure, walking in the backyard. When I told
Mom that Dad was visiting us, she was open and curious, and as I
shared, with conviction, that I knew he was present, the hat Dad
wore daily, hanging securely in its spot in the hallway, fell off the
hook. Dad's first sign. We both knew he was with us and felt reassured. A gentle peace came to both of us.

The day of his funeral was incredibly powerful for my whole family. My husband and I and our three children surrounded Dad in his casket and talked to him in his physical form for the last time. My children, all school age, had written their Grandpa letters, and as we stuffed them into his pocket, we asked him to send us a sign that he was still with us. We ached and longed to see him again, and we told him so. The good-bye was more difficult than I had imagined.

My dad, Marlie, loved to hunt. He grew up on a farm and nature spoke deeply to him. We asked him to come back as a hawk, falcon, or eagle. We wanted so much to have a concrete sign that he was still with us. We then joined the rest of my family for his funeral procession. I felt a wonderful ease that day, surrounded by family, friends, and many guardian angels. It happened to be my birthday: a painful yet transformative way to mark my own passage into my forties.

The next day, my family and I left for a vacation at a family Bible camp in northern Wisconsin, which we had been attending for ten years. We proceeded to lose ourselves in camp activities, but I still carried a longing for my dad. I was consoled knowing I would have a week in the company of caring families with whom I could mourn, pray, and slowly regroup. On the first day of camp we were told that a man who trains birds was planning to visit and share with us. He had never visited the camp before, nor has he since. We were open and curious. Many of us went to see him that warm summer day. He had a beautiful falcon on his arm. We watched his bird soar with incredible grace. One of the kids shouted, "What is your bird's name?" He replied, "Marlie." We were stunned. Marlie! His name was Marlie! We knew in that moment that Dad was with us.

Peace Be With You

Kenneth Lyerly

A week later his disciples were again in the house,
and Thomas was with them. Although the doors
were shut Jesus came and stood among them and
said, "Peace be with you." (v. 26)

When my mother called the last time to tell us that Dad was in the hospital again, and not doing well, I knew we had to go home. I wanted to be there with him and Mom. The doctor let us know right away that Dad wouldn't make it out of the hospital this time. I sat by his bed, holding his hand as he struggled with great pain. At night, I prayed that God would take him soon, for Mom's sake as well as for Dad's, because I could tell how hard it was for her to see him suffer. We were with him when he died the next day, and his last words to each of us were, "I love you." I don't remember more than two other times in my whole life when he said that to me.

As we talked with the pastor about the service, I told him that I felt a very strong need to speak at Dad's funeral. His illness had caused memory lapses, bluntness, and sometimes even cruelty in his relationships with family and friends, and I didn't want people to be left with that impression of him. I wanted everyone to remember him as I did. For two days, I struggled with what I would say. I wanted to express how much Dad meant to me, and I wanted it to be perfect; a trait I had inherited from him. I studied several scripture passages, hoping for an inspiration, but my mind was blocked and time was running short. Finally I tossed the Bible onto the bed and took a break.

When I returned to the bedroom later, still struggling with my thoughts, I saw my father sitting on the bed, and I heard a voice say, "It's okay." It was a brief sensation; natural and not frightening at all. I walked over and picked up the Bible, which had fallen open to Proverbs when I tossed it onto the bed. The passage read:

> *Listen, children, to a father's instruction, and be attentive, that you may gain insight; for I give you good precepts: do not forsake my teaching. When I was a son with my father, tender, and my mother's favorite, he taught me, and said to me, "Let your heart hold fast my words; keep my commandments, and live."*
> — Proverbs 4:1-5

This scripture opened to me the memories of my father that I cherished the most; his self-education; how he had risen from being a grade school dropout to hold an engineer's position before he retired; his love of books and the way he had encouraged us to learn. These were the things I wanted others to know and remember about him. They were the thoughts and memories I would share the next day.

Editor's Note: A longer version of this story appeared under the title, "Opening the Scriptures" in *Lectionary Stories: Forty Tellable Tales for Cycle A*, John Sumwalt, CSS Publishing Company, 1992, pp. 72-74.

Startled

Elaine H. Klemm-Grau

While they were talking about this, Jesus himself
stood among them and said to them, "Peace be
with you." They were startled and terrified, and
thought they were seeing a ghost. (vv. 36b-37)

Jackie was gone. My dear friend and neighbor, to whom I had
ministered in the last six months of her dying, had finally been
released from her pain and had been taken to her true home in
heaven. At home, following the funeral Mass, my heart was heavy
with grief. I laid down and closed my eyes, slipping into contem-
plative prayer.

Then, I was startled by the most beautiful voice I have ever
heard. "Good morning," she said. The voice, though truly indescribable, sounded as pure as the ringing of a lovely bell.

"Who are you?" I replied in amazement. My eyes remained
closed in prayer, and I saw a vision of the profile of a lovely woman
with a flawless complexion and a head covering of blue and white.
"Who are you?" I asked again. The vision faded and I saw two
words, "Mother — Mother."

Talking with my spiritual director about it, I asked him what
"Mother — Mother" meant. He assured me that it would be revealed to me. The next day in class at the seminary, the professor
wrote on the board, "Mother — Mother," and followed it with the
explanation, "Mother of the Redeemer, Mother of Us." The whole
experience gave me a great sense of peace and increased devotion
to the Mother of God. It helped me deal with my sadness over
losing my friend, and strengthened my belief that she was truly
with God.

A few days later, I dreamed of seeing a large, misty, gray sheet,
which appeared more like a very large scroll. Suddenly, the lower

corner was lifted up and peeking around the edge of the scroll-sheet was Jackie, eyes sparkling and smiling. She said, "I'm here!" and the dream ended. I awoke, feeling faith-filled, peaceful, and happy for her arrival at her true home, with God.

God Restores My Soul

John Sumwalt

... he restores my soul, he leads me in right paths for his name's sake. Even though I walk through the darkest valley, I will fear no evil; for you are with me; your rod and your staff — they comfort me. (vv. 3-4)

A few weeks ago, I started reading a psalm a day as part of my daily devotions. I use my old study Bible from Disciple classes, so when I come to a passage that touches me I underline it, then go back and meditate on it for a while before I begin my prayer time.

When I came to day 23 I thought, what can I possibly learn from the twenty-third psalm? I know it by heart. I recite it at the bedsides of the ill and the dying. I read it or hear it read at almost every funeral, partly because I think it is one of the most comforting texts one can read at a funeral, but mostly because when I ask people what scriptures they would like to have read in the service, almost everyone says, "Oh, the Twenty-third Psalm. Mother loved the Twenty-third Psalm."

For most of us, Psalm 23 is the most familiar and most loved passage of scripture. So, I began to read, doubtful that I would learn anything new from something I knew so well.

The Lord is my shepherd
I shall not want,
He makes me to lie down in green pastures,
He leads me beside still waters;
He restores my soul.

I stopped reading. I reached for my pen and I underlined, "He restores my soul." I thought to myself, there has been many a day when I needed my soul restored: some days when the essence of me seemed so broken, so wounded, that I wondered if I could ever be whole again. But somehow, in ways that are still mysterious and wondrous to me, God had touched me and healed me. I whispered a prayer, "Thank you, God, for restoring my soul."

I began to think about soul, to meditate on that part of ourselves we call our souls, to ponder what exactly we are referring to when we talk about soul, and what it is that occurs when God restores one's soul.

Most of us believe that we are more than a physical body. Some discover this when they have an out-of-body experience. A number of years ago, a friend of mine named Agnes had open heart surgery. Agnes loved to talk, and after the operation, when she was home and feeling better, she regaled anyone who would listen with stories about her operation. She said that sometime after the operation began, she found herself floating outside her body near the ceiling. She could see everything that was going on in the operating room. And afterward, to the amazement of the nurses and doctors, she was able to describe everything they had done. She was able to tell the doctor what he was wearing, even though she had not seen him before going under the anesthetic. Was that her soul that left her body for a time and returned after the operation?

Nurses and hospice workers who care for the dying often report being aware when the soul leaves the body. Some tell of an ethereal wispy light that passes from the body into the air above.

Some who have doubts about the existence of an eternal soul have been suddenly convinced when the spirit of a departed one appears to them, as Jesus appeared to his followers after his death. We celebrated the life of Violet Anderson a few weeks ago. Violet was 91 years old. She has been a member of this congregation since 1952. Shortly after she moved to Milwaukee, her beloved son, Edward, died tragically at the age of sixteen. Violet told later how she cried every day for a year. She got up early to visit her son's grave at 6 a.m. every day before she went to work. She cried so much that her tear ducts dried up and she had to receive special treatment. Then one morning, Violet awoke and saw Edward standing at the foot of her bed. He said, "Mom, you've got to stop this crying. I am where I am. I am happy where I am and nothing is going to change it." From that moment on Violet was better. She was able to go on with her life. Her soul had been restored.

We know about restoration of old human-made things: buildings and cars and furniture. Jo and I took a reupholstering class once. We worked on an old, overstuffed chair. Jo made it look pretty good. I tried to stay out of the way. We have several pieces of furniture in our home that Jo has restored: dressers and tables, and an old, upright piano that came from the Odd Fellows Hall in Janesville. Jo spent about 300 hours bringing it back to life. You can still see burn marks in the wood by the keyboard where the piano players at Saturday night dances put out their cigarette stubs. There was no way to remove the marks without further damaging the wood, and we decided they gave character to the piece and thus made it even more dear to us, and perhaps more valuable for resale.

Is that what it's like when a soul is restored? Are there some marks that never come out, that add eternal character and value? The disciples knew something of this when the resurrected Jesus showed them his scarred hands and side.

George Elvey wrote of it in his great Easter hymn, "Crown Him With Many Crowns": "... Crown him the Lord of love; behold his hands and side, those wounds yet visible above, in beauty glorified...."

Whatever the soul is, what effects a soul here on earth, what touches, wounds, strengthens, uplifts, heals, or restores us is carried into eternity.

Excerpted from a sermon preached on September 24, 2000, at Wauwatosa Avenue United Methodist Church in Wauwatosa, Wisconsin.

Shared Power

Robert Maeglin

Then an angel of the Lord said to Philip, "Get up
and go toward the south to the road that goes down
from Jerusalem to Gaza." (v. 26)

It had been a long day of meetings, and a group of scientists were returning from Manila to Los Banos in the Philippines. I, an American, sat with four Filipino men on the forty-mile trip. The driver, a young man called Cata, began to tell a story. It was an amazing story of survival in the mountains of northern Luzon during a typhoon. I listened with rapt attention.

"We were coming down the mountain road when suddenly the mountainside slid across the road, blocking us," Cata said. "It was dark from the rain and strong wind. We stopped just short of the mass of sliding mud and rock. The driver began to back up when we discovered a slide behind us. We were trapped!"

Cata went on to tell how they sat for three days on that mountainside without food, drinking water from the rain that beat against them. The typhoon pounded the vehicle and they wondered when the mountain would slide down on them. Finally, after three days and nights in the vehicle, Cata and a sixty-year-old man decided to go for help.

"We climbed the mountain, above the slides, and planned to cross the mountain beyond the slides and then go down to the highway below," Cata told.

"As we were traversing the side of the mountain, through the broken stones and mud, my foot became trapped and I fell down. I heard a rumbling and looked up at a huge boulder rolling directly at me. I was in complete panic. I struggled to get free, but without success. I screamed at the top of my voice, 'Jesus, help me!' Just above me sat a grapefruit-sized rock. The boulder rolled to a stop at that rock, and the old man jerked me loose as the boulder rolled right over the spot where I was trapped."

Being a Christian, I was spellbound by this story of calling on Jesus. Chills ran up my back and arms as he continued to talk.

He said that he and the old man continued to grope their way across the mountain, stumbling and shivering in the cold fifty-degree temperatures of the storm. The winds, he said, were brutal, the rain pounding them unmercifully. After miles of walking, and at times almost crawling, the old man called to Cata, "I can't go any further. Leave me here. I'll just have to die on the mountain. I'm too weak to go on."

Cata said he once again cried out as loud as possible, "Jesus, help us!"

He then said that he turned his head to see a small "Japanese-looking" woman coming out of the pounding storm. She walked to the old man and took him by the arm. She asked for his pack and said, "Trust in Jesus and follow me."

The old man stood and had walked with her for a short distance when she said to him, "Take off your shoes, it will be easier."

"My feet are sore now. They'll be cut to shreds on the rocks if I take off my shoes," the old man said.

Gently the woman affirmed him, "Trust God and take off your shoes."

I was chilled at the story, listening with excitement.

Cata continued, "The old man walked with a new vigor as the woman led the way down the mountainside, right to a waiting rescue crew. When we arrived at the highway, the old man told me to give the woman some money. I reached in my wallet and turned to give it to the woman, but she was nowhere to be found. It had to be an angel," Cata said.

We drove on into Los Banos and parted, my head full of this "fanciful tale."

A day or so later, I sat at the desk of another scientist at the Forest Products Research and Development Institute in Los Banos, talking to him about a scheduled trip that I had, to go to the Mountain Province in northern Luzon.

Felly said to me, "I had quite an experience up there a couple of months ago in a terrific typhoon."

He began describing exactly what Cata had told a few days before, down to the smallest detail. He told of hearing Cata scream out of the howling wind when he was trapped in the rocks, and how the boulder stopped for an instant after Cata called on Jesus for help. Then Felly grew very quiet and began relating how he knew that he was going to die on the mountain. He said his feet were aching, his legs had lost all strength, and his will was gone. When Cata hollered the second time for Jesus' help, Felly said he had given up hope. Then, to see this woman coming out of the misty storm, he thought he had already died. He told how the woman touched his arm and strength returned to him immediately.

"This little woman, who was smaller than me [Felly stands about five feet tall] lifted me up, taking my pack. She seemed immensely strong. We walked a little way when she said to me, 'Take off your shoes, it will be easier.' "

"My feet are sore now. They'll be cut to shreds on the rocks if I take off my shoes," I replied.

She told me, "Trust God and take off your shoes."

"I did, and I walked without any problem. Over rocks that had even cut into my shoes, I walked without cutting my feet. It was almost like walking on air," Felly said. "When Cata, the woman, and I got to the road, there was a rescue party. I turned to Cata and told him to give the woman some money, because I didn't have any with me. When Cata turned to give the woman the money, she couldn't be found."

Felly looked at me, I suppose wondering if I believed him. Then he said, "I believe that the woman was either Mary or an angel."

Coming to Los Banos a couple of days earlier, I wasn't sure I believed Cata, but now there was no doubt in my mind. The details were exact, the whole story was exact.

Later, as I was on that trip to the Mountain Province, the driver stopped on the rugged, steep mountainside and told me how he, Cata, Felly, and another man were trapped for three days before Cata and Felly left for help. He said that he and the other man stayed in the vehicle for another day and a half before the rescuers arrived. He also told, with detailed exactness, how it all started and what Cata and Felly had told him. "They were saved by an angel. We were all saved by an angel!" he said.

I walked to the edge of the road and looked down, perhaps a thousand feet into the valley below. Then I turned and looked up at the rugged, slide-ridden mountainside above, where, in a blinding typhoon-driven storm, two men experienced God's shared power and mercy.

Dorothy's Story

Dorothy Kraemer

As the Father has loved me, so I have loved you;
abide in my love. If you keep my commandments,
you will abide in my love, just as I have kept my
Father's commandments and abide in his love. I
have said these things to you so that my joy may
be in you, and that your joy may be complete.
(vv. 9-11)

One evening, when I was 26 years old, beleaguered by guilt for acknowledged sins, I was deep into an hour long prayer of repentance. In despair, I grieved that I had broken the commandments and that I was not worthy of God's love.

Near me lay the Bible, unused and unfamiliar. I had never, ever read from the Bible. Yet my hands reached out and took the Bible to open it. I knew not where, nor why. But my hands knew the way. They opened to John 15:9-11 and as my eyes began to read, my mind knew the meaning with clarity. My eyes read verse 10 first: "If you keep my commandments, you will abide in my love, just as I have kept my Father's commandments and abide in his love."

Next I saw verse 9: "As the Father has loved me, so I have loved you; abide in my love."

Then I continued with verse 11: "I have said these things to you so that my joy may be in you, and that your joy may be complete."

Even as I was assimilating this message, I became distinctly aware of a Presence. I marveled at this feeling and my awareness became intense. Fearing that the Presence would not be real, I dared to lift my eyes from the Bible. The Presence remained and lifted my spirit until I felt an inner gladness that was wonderful.

The Presence itself was vague and human-size. I could not see it, though I looked directly at it and knew it was there. The effect of the Presence was all around me.

Still testing the reality, I looked at the Bible and read the verses of John 15:9-11 again. I tried to read verses 12 and 13 or verse 8, then verse 12 again, but those words were blurred to my vision. My eyes could see only verses 9, 10, and 11, so I reread these verses again in the order they had been presented to me, to accept and instill what I recognized as an answer to my prayers. And still the Presence was around me, absolute. I knew it was Jesus, absolutely.

My perception of the Presence remained with me for several minutes after Jesus was gone. My conception of joy was sustained.

This event changed my life. I never again have questioned whether I am forgiven. I feel secure in God's love. I trust the Spirit of Jesus' presence. I believe and trust in prayer. I try to have my prayers include listening. I live life with a comprehension of the wonder.

As I have read and studied the Bible in the many years beyond this episode, the same message seems clearly evident for all who read to see, for those who pray to know, and for all who love to be.

Through some years of spiritual drought, when I searched in vain for relief in prayer, and through a long depression, when I liked myself less and less, I never did lose my faith. That in itself is part of the wonder. I remember the Presence I knew and the gift message I had received.

We can know God loves us. We can trust God hears our prayers. We can feel the presence of Jesus, and so we can live in joy.

Dorothy Kraemer was a long time, faithful member of Wauwatosa Avenue United Methodist Church in Milwaukee. This story, written in her own words, was read at her memorial service at the church on September 1, 1995. It first appeared in *Lectionary Tales for the Pulpit: 62 Stories for Cycle B*, John Sumwalt and Joanne Perry-Sumwalt, CSS Publishing Company, 1996, pp. 108-111.

Convincing Proof

Margaret Nyland-Brown

After his suffering, he presented himself alive to them by many convincing proofs, appearing to them during forty days and speaking about the kingdom of God. (v. 3)

I was born in 1970. My brother, Randy, was five years older than I. He died on February 28, 1982. In February of 1992, Randy came to me in a dream. At the time that I had this experience, I would have been a senior in college. I had been struggling with issues of whether we have a soul, and whether my brother was in a special place.

I dreamed that I was in a snow-covered field, but I wasn't cold. I saw Randy and suddenly I felt very tired and lay down on the ground and went to sleep. Sometime later, I awoke in the field and I looked up and saw him still standing there, watching me. We looked at each other for what seemed like a long time. I saw his face so clearly. He was wearing something red.

I tried to get up, but I couldn't. I called out his name and said, "Wait just a minute." But he turned and walked away, and disappeared. A few seconds later, I saw a bunch of moving lights in the shape of a body rise up, until it looked like a constellation against the stars in the night sky. Then he whizzed away overhead. I reached out my hand to wave, and I saw his hand raised as he zoomed out of sight.

The overwhelming feeling that I remember from this vivid experience is that of utter peace washing over me: of warmth, of love, not just his love for me, but something much bigger. Without the exchange of words, I received a message that everything was all right. It was so very comforting.

Pentecost

I asked the light, "If you leave me now, is there a place I can go and find you?" "I am always near those from whom people hide their faces. Find them and you find me ... I am the one who hides that you may find me."

Eddie Ensley

Eddie Ensley, *Visions: The Soul's Path to the Sacred* (Chicago: Loyola Press, 2000), p. 28.

My Encounter With God

Robert L. Gossett

*All of them were filled with the Holy Spirit and
began to speak in other languages, as the Spirit
gave them ability.* (v. 4)

A United Methodist pastor, lying on a Lutheran gymnasium
floor, struggling with God about speaking in tongues is not something you would expect to see very often, but that is a part of my
story. That incident took place in about 1974, and it is still an important part of my spiritual life. A little background might be help-
ful in understanding it.

I grew up in the Evangelical United Brethren Church, which
merged in 1968 with the Methodist Church to form the United
Methodist Church. Sunday School, Youth Fellowship, and other
church activities were always an important part of my life. Five
years after I graduated from high school, I entered college with the
intention of becoming a pastor. There was no dramatic call from
God at that time; just awareness on my part and that of others that
this seemed to be a place where I could serve.

My search for a deeper experience of God may have been
present for some time, but I became more aware of it as I saw in
some lay people an awareness and experience of God that I knew I
didn't have. They talked about a personal relationship with Jesus,
and being filled or baptized with the Holy Spirit, which made their
faith alive and vital. They sometimes offered books, tapes, invita-
tions to prayer groups, or special speakers, which answered some
of my questions and further heightened my interest. My biggest
question was about speaking in tongues. I had heard it at a youth
prayer meeting once, and I had done a lot of reading about it, but I
wasn't sure I wanted anything to do with it.

My interest in these topics culminated one night following a Bible study at church. I asked several of the lay people to pray for me concerning my questions and desire for a deeper relationship with Jesus and experience of the Holy Spirit. I knelt at the altar while they placed their hands on my head and shoulders and prayed for me. There were no flashing lights, visions, speaking in tongues, or anything like that, but I could tell I was changed. The Bible came to life in ways that it hadn't before; my preaching became more positive and Christ-centered; prayer became more exciting; and the desire to share my faith became more intense. It was a major turning point in my faith, but God wasn't done with me yet.

Several months later, my wife and I went to St. Louis to visit former members of our church who had moved there. An evangelist with a healing ministry was speaking, so we all decided to go. Following her sermon, the evangelist invited people to come forward to accept Jesus and receive prayer for healing or any other need. Many people went forward for prayer. As some received prayer, they fell to the floor. We had never experienced that before and thought it was a little strange, but it happened to a United Methodist pastor and a young boy, among many others, so we didn't question its validity. We learned later that it was called "being Slain in the Spirit," as people came under the power of the Spirit. My own encounter with the Spirit was drawing closer.

Later that summer, my wife and I went to a Lutheran gymnasium to hear a couple who had become Christians later in life and wondered why everyone wasn't as excited about the Christian faith as they were. They had written a number of books, which I had read, so I wanted to hear them in person. Following their presentation, they invited people to come forward for prayer to receive Jesus, be filled with the Holy Spirit, and receive prayer for healing or other special needs. Two long lines formed, one for the husband, one for the wife, and Jeri and I got into the line to see the wife. When we got to her, I told her that I was a United Methodist pastor, and that I wanted more of the power she had been talking about. She asked me if I had received the Baptism in the Holy Spirit, and I said that I believed I had. She asked if I spoke in tongues, and I said that I had a lot of questions about it and problems with it. She placed her hand on my shoulder in prayer, and the next thing I knew, I was down on the gym floor. Jeri didn't know what to do, and the evangelist said, "Don't help him; he's under the power of God."

I'm not exactly sure what I was experiencing and feeling on that gym floor, but I'm sure I was struggling with God. I have no concept of the amount of time I was there, but when I got up, Jeri and I talked to the speaker again. She asked me if I had spoken in tongues; I said no and that I still had a lot of questions and problems with it. She said, "Just try it." I told her I had, but nothing came out. She said, "You know what's going to happen if you don't?" And then I was on the floor again, struggling with God and my questions and fears about speaking in tongues. Again, I don't know how long I was there. Jeri went to the bleachers to sit with some friends. They told me later that they had been praying, "Knock him silly, Lord." I think their prayers were answered.

As I lay on the floor, a word or phrase came to mind which I didn't understand. I don't know if I thought it or said it, but it was the beginning of a new prayer language, which has become part of my new prayer life. It is something I use regularly as an expression of praise to an awesome God or when I pray for a situation in which I'm not sure what the specific need is. I use it often throughout the day in my private expressions of praise and prayer, and use it only rarely with another person or group.

When I share this experience, I always say that this does not make me better than anyone who has not experienced it. I can only say that it has made my personal awareness of God much deeper and my desire to serve God greater. The power of God is awesome. Your experience may take you down a different path, but don't be afraid of seeking and accepting all God has for you.

Born Of The Spirit

Earl Kammerud

Do not be astonished that I said to you, "You must be born from above." The wind blows where it chooses, and you hear the sound of it, but you do not know where it comes from or where it goes. So it is with everyone who is born of the Spirit. (vv. 7-8)

I attended a Billy Graham Evangelism workshop in 1982. I didn't know, when I signed up and accepted scholarship money for the workshop, that there was an obligation also to attend his evening meetings in typical Graham style. At the end of the first night, after Graham's invitation to come forward, a voice spoke to me, "Earl, it is time to go down." I was shocked! Another voice answered, "He doesn't need to go down." I didn't move and tried to ignore this happening.

The next night, after the invitation, the first voice spoke again, "Earl, you need to go down. You may not have another opportunity." Again, the second voice answered, in a sarcastic tone, "That's crazy. Why should he go down?" But this time I got up and started moving through the large convention hall, through the foyer, into the auditorium to get finally to the floor in front of Graham. All this time I was crying tears of joy and relief. A heavy load was lifted from me. And at the same time, my second voice kept trying to persuade me not to do what I was doing. I was met in front of the podium by a young man with a Gospel of John in his hand. He started to show me Jesus' steps to salvation, then he asked me what I did. When I said I was a United Methodist clergy person, he replied, "Well, we don't have to finish this." And I replied, "Don't leave one step out."

This was a turning point in my ministry and life. I would like to say everything was better after that. However, it seems like I have been tempted more and buffeted more, yet have been stronger to continue the fight for justice.

Just Let Go

Bonny J. Bailey

As we work together with him, we urge you also
not to accept the grace of God in vain. For he says,
"At an acceptable time I have listened to you, and
on a day of salvation I have helped you." See, now
is the acceptable time; see, now is the day of sal-
vation! (vv. 1-2)

My first husband was an alcoholic, which made for a very rough marriage. We had four children and I wanted to stay together. I tried to do everything I could to make him happy and to make the marriage work. Despite this, it wasn't working.

One night, after yet another of our arguments, I sat on the stairs leading to our basement. There were no lights on, and no nearby windows, just brick walls surrounding me. I felt as though I was at the bottom of a pit. I put my head down and cried, pleading with God, "Lord, I just can't take this anymore. I don't know what else to do; I've tried everything to keep this marriage going. Please help me. You've got to tell me what to do!"

All of a sudden, I felt like someone had placed a hand on my shoulder and all the heavy weight was being lifted off my back. As that weight was lifted, I looked up and saw a glowing light in the middle of the room. As I looked into the light, I heard a voice in my head saying, "Just let go, everything will be all right."

I stood up feeling very relaxed, and then went back upstairs and told my husband to do what he wanted to do. I then went to bed and had the best sleep that I had in a long time. I ended up getting a divorce. It was rough at times, but everything ended up for the best.

116

I believe God was telling me that I was trying too hard to control too many things. I just had to let go and let him take over in my life. Through the years I have been guided by that voice, only without the light. I have grown to trust in the Lord with all my heart. I know he is in charge, not me.

Overcome With Amazement

Jean Hodge, as told to John Sumwalt

... he said to them, "Why do you make a commotion and weep? The child is not dead but sleeping." And they laughed at him. Then he put them all outside, and took the child's father and mother and those who were with him, and went in where the child was. He took her by the hand and said to her, "Talitha cum" which means, "Little girl, get up!" And immediately the little girl got up and began to walk about (she was twelve years of age). At this they were overcome with amazement. (vv. 39b-42)

Pastor Tom Hodge was about to leave his office to go home for supper when he received word that one of his members was in the hospital and was not expected to live. He called his wife, Jean, to tell her he was going to be late, and set out for the hospital. When he arrived he found the man's family crying and embracing each other in the corridor outside the room. The doctor had just announced to them that their loved one had died.

Pastor Hodge asked if he could go into the room. There were several more members of the family gathered around the bed. He said to them, "Any of you who don't know the Lord, you leave this room." Then he went over to the bed, laid his hands on the man and prayed. The man opened his eyes and looked up. The family was elated and the hospital staff were amazed.

The man lived for about a week before he became ill again. This time the Lord took him home for good. But in that week of extra life, he received the Lord as his personal savior. And many who witnessed this miracle also gave their lives to Christ.

On another occasion a couple came to Pastor Hodge with a baby that was not expected to live. The child had a bowel obstruction for which nothing could be done in those days. The pastor took the baby in his arms and prayed for healing. The couple called later with great excitement to report that the child's bowels had moved and he would be all right.

Tom Hodge served Assembly of God Churches for over fifty years in West Bend, Hartford, and Mather, Wisconsin, and in Ishpeming, Michigan. He died in 1998. His wife, Jean Hodge, who is ninety, and now lives in a retirement home near West Bend, tells how her husband has sometimes appeared next to her in bed at night. She said, "One night he came to me, and put his hand on my shoulder, and I went to put my hand on his hand, and his hand slipped away. I just couldn't get over it because he was right there, and he smiled at me. He was comforting me. I felt so elated. It was just so wonderful. I know he is with the Lord."

Caught Up Into Paradise

And I know that such a person — whether in the
body or out of the body I do not know; God knows
— was caught up into Paradise and heard things
that are not to be told, that no mortal is permitted
to repeat. (vv. 3-4)

Lee E. Meissner

He was an average-size man with a deep bass voice that reminded you of Harold of the Statler Brothers. He had sung in the church choir and a men's quartet for many years. He was a caring and loving man, and a Christian in the best sense of the word. If asked to give his testimony at a worship service, he would do it only after much arm twisting. He preferred to live his love for God rather than speak it. He did a good job of influencing many lives by his lifestyle and his actions. I think it was his smile and kind words that were most noticeable.

In his mid-eighties, he started to experience a number of health problems. He would get one ailment under control only to have another arise. His deep bass voice was no longer strong and vibrant, and the day finally came when he was admitted to the hospital for the last time. The doctors told his family that he would soon die.

For whatever reason, the children wanted a detailed account of just how their dad's last days would be. They wanted an hour by hour account. When would he no longer know them? When would he go into a coma, or would he? The doctors complied and gave them updates each day of what to expect. His health continued to deteriorate.

I remember visiting him every day of the last week of his life. He was at a point where it was an effort for him to do anything. He could sort of get that smile, but it was an effort. He could say a few words, but only a few.

On the day before he died, I went into his room and was amazed at what I saw. He glowed like one of those fluorescent key chains after the lights go out. His smile was back, his voice strong and deep. As soon as he saw me, he said, "Pastor, it was wonderful. I was there last night. I was in heaven and it is the most beautiful place I have ever seen. And I am going there forever tonight." He went on to tell of the beauty of heaven. On that day, he was as excited as a kid with a new toy. Then he thanked me for our friendship through the years and said that he would be leaving that night. The next morning I received word that he had died.

The family heard this story over and over all day as people visited their father. For some reason, he had many more visitors than usual. Each person heard the story of heaven. Each of them saw the glow that encircled him. All of the nurses, and any of the other hospital staff who saw him that day, heard the same story. The doctors said it was just a matter of hallucination.

Before and after the funeral, those who had visited him asked me what I thought of his vision. I told them I believed every word he said. His vision of heaven helped many people accept his death and took some of the fear of death from them ... but not the doctors.

The man's name was Burr Hilvers, and he lived in Cuba City, Wisconsin, for most of his life.

Ena Minckler

I had a minor operation in 1976, and sometime during the three hours while they were trying to bring me to, I left my body and went up through a black hole. It was a long way up, but I was through it in no time. Still, I did not feel like I was moving fast.

I had a feeling of very great love. I'm sure I was in heaven. The love was more than a mother feels for her children. I saw adult people moving around. The light was just right. There were no shadows anywhere from anything. I'm sure it was "God's light." I did not want to come back. To this day I can still feel the love.

121

The Mystery Of His Will

Marcia Lee

... he has made known to us the mystery of his will, according to his good pleasure that he set forth in Christ, as a plan for the fullness of time, to gather up all things in him, things in heaven and things on earth. (vv. 9-10)

There was a time, when my children were all in school, when my life seemed meaningless. Everything I did was undone by the end of the day. The meals I prepared were either eaten or rejected. The house I cleaned got messed up. The clothes I washed and folded became dirty and scattered all over the floor. Everyone in my family was aspiring to become something. They were growing. I was standing still, facilitating other people's lives, but not having a life of my own. This was not what I had expected to be doing when I grew up.

One morning, I got up and managed to get dressed, but found that I had no idea what to do. Nothing was worth the effort. At the bedroom door, I didn't know whether to turn to the right or to the left. Should I sit on the sofa or stand in the kitchen? I didn't even know what to do with the next ten minutes, let alone the rest of the day, so I went back to bed.

Eventually, I decided to go for a walk and put the matter before God. It was my intention to wander aimlessly in the woods until I found a direction. It had snowed during the night. The sky was blue and the morning was crisp and bright. Juniper branches drooped, laden with snow. Sage and Rabbit Brush were white lumps on the landscape. Tracks of small creatures made lacy patterns in the snow. Behind me, I could see where my own less delicate feet had plowed a trail through the woods.

Suddenly, the sun gleamed brilliantly on the snow. To my amazement, I caught the sight of the crystalline formations of individual snowflakes. It had always been my presumption that snow stars could only be seen under a microscope or with the aid of some other visual enhancer, but there I was, looking at millions of individual snowflakes with my naked eyes. When I swooshed my hand through the powder, perfect, fragile stars clung to my black glove and scattered themselves all over my coat. This was absolutely mesmerizing to me, and I have no idea how long I remained there.

Then, in an instant, I knew what I was supposed to be doing with my life: jillions and jillions of little things, fragile passing things, things which are everywhere and cover everything, things which nobody can even see unless the sun happens to gleam on them just right!

I have never forgotten that moment, and it has inspired me many times since. It has given meaning to my work, my relationships with people, my days, and my life in general. I feel so grateful for the lovely way that God spoke to me that day.

Someone To Watch Over Me

Forever I will keep my steadfast love for him, and
my covenant with him will stand firm. (v. 28)

Patricia M. Thaker

In February of 2000, my grandfather, Lloyd Dings, was diagnosed with pancreatic cancer. He passed away just twelve days later. My grandparents were married 56 years. The legacy he leaves behind is a wonderful wife and a beautiful family

On the afternoon he died, I sat by Grandfather's side and had a brief conversation with him. We held hands and I cried as we spoke. I told him that I did not want him to leave us, and he replied that he knew, but he had to. I asked him to promise to watch over me when he was gone, and he promised that he would. I also asked him to be with me on my wedding day, to which he replied that he'd try his hardest.

He died six hours later.

That evening, I returned to my parents' home and fell sleep in the basement my grandfather had designed and built. About four hours later I woke, terrified to realize I couldn't move. I had a strong sense that my grandfather was present and standing at the end of the couch looking over me. A cool whisper passed across my face. I tried to make sense of what was happening, but couldn't. Minutes later, I saw tiny white lights in front of me, and the sensation passed. Finally I could move again. I looked behind me, expecting to see my grandfather, but he wasn't there. I looked at the place I had sensed him to be and kept repeating, "I love you, Grandpa, I love you Grandpa." I glanced at the clock, and it was 2:02 a.m. Still somewhat frightened, I turned on all the lights and the television. Eventually I fell back asleep.

The next morning, confused and grief stricken, I spoke with my mother about my experience. Later, we went to my grandmother Kathryn Ding's home, and we discovered something amazing. She had felt his presence at the same time I had.

My grandmother was sleeping in the bed they had shared for so many years, and where my grandfather had died. She awoke feeling as if there was a cloud hovering over her. Rather than feeling frightened, she was comforted by this presence. But she wasn't sure exactly what it meant until I shared my story.

Later that day, I spoke with Alex, my fiance, and shared with him what had happened the night before. At that point, I still could not talk about it without crying. He listened and tried to comfort me. Then Alex told me that the strangest thing had happened to him the night before. He stirred in bed and awoke with a feeling that something was moving about the room. He quickly told himself that it must be the cat, then realized the cat was asleep next to him. We discovered that this occurred near the same time my grandmother and I had our experiences.

Sometimes I lay awake at night and say, "Okay, Grandpa, you can come back and visit me again."

He hasn't, yet, but I know I'll always have him watching over me.

Editor's Note: Lloyd M. Dings was a longtime, faithful member of Wauwatosa Avenue United Methodist Church, where I serve as pastor. I visited with Lloyd in his home the day before he died. His whole extended family and a few friends were gathered in the living room. Lloyd was holding court in his recliner in the study. Kathryn was taking one or two people in at a time, so as not to tire him. When my turn came, I observed that Lloyd was weak, but his spirit was as strong as ever. We talked about many things. It was apparent that Lloyd had made his peace with everyone in this world, that he had finished his work here and was prepared to die with complete trust in God. He said, "I have my faith." As we were finishing our conversation, and as I was preparing to invite the others to come in and join us in prayer, Lloyd said, "John, I have a question for you. When I see my parents, what will they look like?

Will they appear old as they were when they died, or will they appear as they were when they were younger?" I shared what I have read in several sources, that people in their spirit bodies generally appear as they were in their prime. But, I admitted that I do not know for sure. I said, "Lloyd, why don't you come back and tell me." Then, I told him that it is possible that he would be able to visit his loved ones after he died, and perhaps be able to communicate with them as Jesus communicated with his disciples after his resurrection.

Kathryn Taughinbaugh

My grandma, Dorothy Taughinbaugh, passed away in 1995, when I was in third grade. It came as a complete shock to me and my family. After she died, almost every Sunday I would pray to God during our silent prayer time, asking to hear her voice one last time.

In August of 2001, just before my sophomore year in high school, I went on my first church mission trip to an Indian reservation in Red Lake, Minnesota. It was very calm and peaceful there, and we had a worship service every night. In the last worship service, during our prayer time, I heard a familiar voice. It didn't sound like the guy who was leading the prayer. The voice said, "I love you and I am always watching over you." This voice was my grandma's, and when I heard it I started crying and couldn't stop, I was so overwhelmed. I'm so happy that God answered my prayer.

Grounded In Love

Kai M. McClinton

I pray that, according to the riches of his glory, he may grant that you may be strengthened in your inner being with power through his Spirit, and that Christ may dwell in your hearts through faith, as you are being rooted and grounded in love. (vv. 16-17)

My family is very close. We depend on one another and do all that we can for each other. When one is in trouble, we all come running to assist in any way that we can. We learned this kind of love and support from our grandmother, Elsie Burton. She was a hard working woman who loved her family and all people.

My grandmother passed away in 1991, from a heart attack. It was a shock to all who knew her. Mama, as I called her, was the rock. She was the foundation of our family, and when she died, we thought that life was about to end.

One year later, I was working as a telemarketer for Sears and Roebuck. The building was located in a large parking lot, near many garages that housed packing trucks. Our boss constantly reminded us to be careful when we walked through the parking lot, because the trucks drove in and out of the garages at a high rate of speed. She didn't want anyone to get hit.

On this particular day, I had been crying over Mama. I was her oldest grandchild, and she and I had been close — stuck like glue — so I really missed her. I had gotten out of my car and was walking toward the telemarketers' building, so lost in my mood that I wasn't paying attention to my surroundings. I approached an open garage door and began to cross in front of it, when I suddenly felt someone grab the back of my shirt and pull me, and I fell back. At that same moment, a big truck came speeding out of the garage, the driver never having seen me.

I turned to thank whoever it was that pulled me back, but there was no one there. My mind told me it could have been my imagination, but my heart knew that someone had pulled me away from danger. Then I saw a button lying on the ground that had popped off my shirt when I was pulled back.

I felt a rush go through me. I was thinking about Mama, and I felt her presence. She was there, protecting me from danger. I thanked God for showing me that even though my grandmother was gone, she was with me in spirit. Since then, I have known that I will never be without my Mama.

God is an awesome God, for he sends angels to protect his children here on earth!

That Which Comes From Heaven

Janet Angel

*Our ancestors ate the manna in the wilderness; as
it is written, "He gave them bread from heaven to
eat." Then Jesus said to them, "Very truly I tell
you, it was not Moses who gave you the bread from
heaven, but it is my Father who gives you the true
bread from heaven. For the bread of God is that
which comes down from heaven and gives life to
the world." They said to him, "Sir, give us this
bread always." (vv. 31-34)*

As a little girl, about five years old, I began to "know" things
before they would happen. I was receiving information and musical pieces without formal education. People sought my advice, even
as a child, because I could channel information to help them. I
experienced a silent dialogue with angels, and then had an appari-
tion of Mary at my bedside at five years of age. I was told that my
life would not be ordinary. I understood that I was supposed to
spread the word of God, but I wasn't sure how. I was instructed not
to discuss what I was receiving until the time was right. For 43
years from my first memory of my silent dialogue with God, I
waited to make public what I was receiving. I began to realize that
we are much like radio stations. When there is little or no static, we
can pick up pure transmission, modulate, and then transmit.

As I grew older, being raised in a Catholic home, I thought that
I was supposed to be a nun, so I went in that direction for a time,
only to be guided away from that role later on. I have a doctorate in
Psychology, because my concrete mind wanted to "prove" what I
was receiving from God. But I later realized that we cannot differ-
entiate between all that we are, being body, mind, and spirit. I was
silently taught about meditation: given incredible wisdom about

our truest nature, the hidden vocabulary in our words, cosmic innate intelligence, how to help people heal themselves, the blueprints of our souls, how to stop our cells from aging, telekinesis, clairvoyance, clairaudience, remote viewing, and much, much more. This dialogue with God continues every day. I awaken at about four o'clock each morning to sit at the computer and receive, then transmit my questions. In my first book, I list questions that I have been asking about our supreme source of light and intelligence and LOVE (God). We are so much more than anyone has ever imagined. Once we perfect our independent lives of all of the illusions on earth and move toward healing, we then will be able to use our innate gifts: those Jesus was trying to teach us (which was attempting the impossible) and eventually we will concern ourselves with collective consciousness, which writes the script for life on earth. To say I feel blessed in receiving this information is understatement. It is a joy I pray that all people will eventually experience for themselves.

My message has been consistent as I continue to receive love from the highest source in existence. Some have believed that God stopped communicating with us as humans during the time of Moses. Well, God did not. I am now in the midst of teaching others, through seminars and writing, how to receive the answers we seek directly from God. There are different forms of communication which are appropriate for each person. My deepest desire is to enlighten as many souls as possible to the truth of our identity and potential from a place of unconditional love.

Janet Angel is the author of *All That You Are: Your True Identity.* See www.amazon.com

Do Not Let The Sun
Go Down On Your Anger

Marjorie K. Evans

Be angry but do not sin; do not let the sun go down
on your anger ... be kind to one another, tender-
hearted, forgiving one another, as God in Christ
has forgiven you. (vv. 26a, 32)

It was a ridiculous quarrel. Later, we couldn't even remember what it was about. But that night, neither my husband Ed nor I wanted to admit we were wrong. So, instead of following the biblical advice of not letting the sun go down on our wrath, we went to bed angry.

Turning my back to him, I thought we would soon go to sleep. But Ed kept tossing restlessly, and I lay there mulling over and over our harsh words to each other. I felt terrible, as if I were forsaken and all alone, and I huddled there, sobbing softly.

Finally Ed said, "Marjorie, why don't we go into the living room and pray?" Eager to do anything to rectify our relationship, I agreed. We knelt beside the coffee table, gave our problems to the Lord, and asked his forgiveness. We then apologized to each other and had a precious time of reconciliation.

We returned to bed and soon fell into a peaceful sleep, but, during the night, every time I turned over, I was aware of a wonderful, spicy fragrance. However, I couldn't wake up enough to find out what it was or where it was coming from.

The next morning, the fragrance was gone. Excitedly, I told Ed, "I think Jesus was here last night, because all night long I smelled an exotic and spicy fragrance, perhaps like incense. It was more fragrant than anything I've ever smelled. And I felt absolutely at peace. I'm sure it was Jesus, comforting us and letting us know he is pleased with us."

"I didn't smell anything, Honey," Ed responded. "But you're more sensitive than I am, so I'm sure you're right. I also had a peaceful night's sleep."

Giving me a big hug and kiss, Ed went on to say, "We serve a wonderful Lord who is concerned about every aspect of our lives. I do know he was pleased when we prayed last night, gave our differences to him, and forgave each other. Truly, he is a rewarder of those who earnestly seek him as well as being the God of all comfort."

What Dreams Have Come

At Gibeon the Lord appeared to Solomon in a
dream by night; and God said, "Ask what I should
give you." (v. 5)

John Sumwalt/Ruth A. Smith

After my father died, in September of 1998, I had several vivid dreams that felt very much like his real presence. These came after weeks of aching for my dad and praying to know he was all right. In one dream I saw him standing by the silo on the farm in his bib overalls. He looked at me with love and I was filled with peace and joy. In another dream I found myself sitting beside him at a family gathering. It was enormously comforting. Once he came to me looking radiant, as I remember him when he was in his late thirties, young and strong and full of life. Each time I woke I felt my prayers had been answered. Dad is doing well.

My daughter, Kati, also had a striking dream just after Dad's death in which her grandfather told her he felt badly about something he had done to my mother. He wanted her to know how sorry he was and how much he loved her. I suggested to Kati that it may have meant that her grandfather was in life review. I suggested she tell her grandmother about the dream.

When I e-mailed my sister, Ruth Smith, about the wonderful comfort I had received from my dreams of Dad, she wrote back, lamenting that she had experienced no sign of his presence. The very next day she wrote to tell me of a dream in which the phone rang during a family gathering at her house. "My husband Bruce answered it and I heard him sound very surprised. He handed the phone to you and you called for me. So I came downstairs, you handed me the phone and it was Dad calling me! He sounded so happy and was cracking jokes. He told me to keep making progress, or something to that effect, and something about my daughter Jessi winning something. And, then I kiddingly said to him, 'Hope you didn't call collect.' He laughed and laughed, and I laughed with him. Then I woke up, and I had the biggest smile on my face, and I was soooo happy!"

Gretchen Kane, a member of our congregation, tells of "a very strong, comforting dream" she had of her father a few months after his death. She said, "I had watched him shrivel up the ten days I was with him in his home before he died. In the dream he walked to me with open arms and hugged me hard. I could feel that he was strong, rested, and happy. It really made me feel better knowing he was whole again."

Sandra Kilbride-Becker, a faithful soul I came to know when I was pastor in Montello, Wisconsin, told me of an unforgettable dream she had after the death of her youngest son.

Sandra Kilbride-Becker

Mike was a fifteen-year-old kid who seemed very healthy and was into sports and all of the things that normal boys do. He had just gotten his first summer job when it was time for our yearly vacation, and he did not want to go with Mom and Dad. We let him stay home with his nineteen-year-old brother and his eighteen-year-old sister, with the provision that they each see their grandmother every day. She lived less than a mile away. We called every night to see if everything was okay.

One bright June morning, just after we arrived in the next town where we were scheduled to stay, we received a call from our older son saying Mike had fallen and they never got to the hospital. Needless to say, we drove home the 350 miles wondering all the way just what had happened. We wanted to get home as quickly as possible, and yet the closer we got the more we dreaded it. We just did not believe anything could have happened to our son. Nothing has ever hurt more. The pain was like a stone on my chest. When we got home there were a lot of people and the police had been through the house. It was one big nightmare, because no one knew what had happened to this child. That night, when I went to bed, I prayed that I could not handle this load on my own, and a feeling of peace came over me. God said that he would help us through this time. A few days later, we learned that Mike died of a birth defect that had not been detected during his life.

Not long after this, God answered my prayers again. Mike had been dead a short while and I was having trouble adjusting. Mike came to me in a dream one morning and said not to cry anymore. He said he was in heaven with God, everything was nice, and no one hurt anymore. He said he was lonesome and he asked God if he could come back and get his dog and his slingshot. A week later the dog died, and we never did find his slingshot.

A Heavenly Voice

Rosmarie Trapp

For a day in your courts is better than a thousand elsewhere. I would rather be a doorkeeper in the house of my God than live in the tents of wickedness. (v. 10)

When I was growing up, in our large family which performed all over Europe and the U.S., I was the rebellious one. I was the one who decided I no longer wanted to sing with the family, and eventually I ran away, causing much grief and pain for everyone. It seems to me that my brain was in total darkness. Once, when it seemed that I had sunk as low as I could sink, I heard an evangelist on a radio program talk about repeating a sinner's prayer to confess to God our need for forgiveness. I said that prayer, asking God's forgiveness by the Blood of the Lamb, and it changed my life. But my mother had also been praying for me, as she prayed for all her children. She was a powerful prayer, and by her faith in God, I came back home safely. Now, more and more, I can see the past in the light of God, and I realize that *he was there all the time.* He really is the Good Shepherd.

Agathe, my oldest sister, had also had a "heavenly experience," and she enthusiastically invited my other sisters and I to a ten-day retreat at an Ann Arbor, Michigan, university. The four of us, Hedwig, Maria, Agathe, and I, all went there. Living in different houses, we would get together for meetings and services. One day, I got tired of all the meetings. They didn't reach my spirit, so I decided to take a walk "to anywhere out in the world."

It was a lovely, warm summer day. I remember walking through a quiet suburb, under sycamore trees, when I heard a booming voice say, "No Man's Land." It came from nowhere. I could pinpoint no radio, no car with a horn blaring out at me. Then, in awe, I decided it must have been God calling to me. The rebellion in my soul made me pretend I had not heard it, and on I went, only to find myself at a dead end, with an empty house on the right side.

That made me think twice about my "running away," because the message that suddenly came to me was: If you keep on, you will be in "no man's land" and become like an abandoned house. Reluctantly, I turned back and found the rest of the members of the retreat in the gym, praising God in tongues, with lifted hands.

It was such a beautiful and peaceful sight! As I had entered upstairs, I could see people from above with lifted hands. Also, people were coming in across the gym, and a scripture popped into my head: "I would rather be a doorkeeper in the house of my God than live in the tents of wickedness." That was the first time this had happened, and I later found out the scripture was from Psalm 84:10. As I seek the Lord, my spirit is quickened by his influence.

Isn't God wonderful to intervene in the choices we make in our lives? He brings us out of darkness into his marvelous light. Those are the only words I can use to express my thanks — my spirit was really in deep darkness, like a pit in the ground that I couldn't get out of myself. God still lifts me out of the pits that I stumble into. He is the Good Shepherd who watches his sheep! Trust in him. He is worthy! Jesus loves you and me!

Editor's Note: Rosmarie von Trapp is the daughter of Captain George and Maria von Trapp whose story was told in the movie, *The Sound of Music*. Rosmarie was the first of three children born to the von Trapps after their marriage. The widowed captain already had seven children when Maria came to be the family governess. Rosmarie and her nine brothers and sisters made up the von Trapp Family singers who became famous after their triumphant flight from Nazi-controlled Austria in the 1930s.

My Beloved

Judie M. Jacobson

The voice of my beloved! Look, he comes, leap-
ing upon the mountains, bounding over the hills.
(v. 8)

Beth and David are a young couple in my congregation who have a wonderful relationship and a tremendous heart for people. One day, while I was working at my desk, I received a phone call from Beth. It turned out to be a rare moment where I was given the opportunity to share my mystical, yet very "real" relationship with God, whom I call "My Beloved."

The night before, she and Dave were coming home from a special event that had given them both great joy, and they were sharing their joy with each other. It occurred to them that, when I went home, I had no one with whom to share my joy. They were concerned for me as a single woman. Beth called to express this concern.

But I told her, "I do! I have God!" She continued by saying that was all well and good, but what did I do when everything seemed to go wrong, and what I really needed was a hug, and there was no one there.

Again, I said, "But I do have someone there! I have God! Let me explain. Many times when I sit quietly in my early morning devotion time, I feel God brush hands down over my hair and kiss my upturned face or the top of my head. When I come home after a long day's work, I never feel that I come into an empty house. God's loving presence is always there to welcome me. When you go to bed at night, with a broken heart or a heavy spirit, you curl up next to your husband and feel comforted. When I go to bed at night, I curl up next to God and feel comforted. I feel arms around me and am surrounded by a strong presence of love! The experience is as 'real' as any human partner's presence could provide.

"Plus," I joked with her, "God knows all my shortcomings and is more patient and understanding than any earthly partner I have ever known. There is no need for you and Dave to be concerned that I may be alone and uncared for. I have My Beloved and it is more than enough!"

Blessed Kateri Tekakwitha

Allan McCauley, as told to Rebecca Henderleiter

Then looking up to heaven, he sighed and said to him, "Ephphatha," that is, "Be opened." And immediately his ears were opened, his tongue was released, and he spoke plainly. (vv. 34-35)

Our four-year-old son, Peter, was suffering from chronic otitis media, a disease of the middle ear that was causing him to go deaf. Two specialists, Dr. Besserman and Dr. Barnett, concurred that the only option to save Peter's hearing would be to implant tubes in his ears surgically. After the surgery, Peter would no longer be allowed to go swimming, which devastated him because he loved the water so much. Living in Arizona, swimming was a part of everyday activities in order to escape the summer heat.

At that time, my wife Marlene and I were involved in setting up lectures in Arizona churches by Reverend Francis X. Weiser, S. J., who had just published a book on the life of Kateri Tekakwitha, a Mohawk-Algonquin virgin who lived between 1656 and 1680. She had been declared "Venerable" by Pope Pius XII in 1943, and "Blessed" by Pope John Paul II in 1980, the first two steps toward sainthood. She will be the first Native American saint.

One day, when Peter, Marlene, and I were picking up Father Weiser at the airport, we were speaking very loudly, nearly shouting so that Peter could hear our conversation.

"Why are you yelling?" Father Weiser asked.

"Our son has a serious ear problem and is nearly deaf," I explained.

"Deafness?" the Father said in his thick German accent. "Then let us ask Kateri to help! She leaves no prayer unanswered!"

We began a nine-day novena, asking Kateri's intercession, as the Father had instructed. On the ninth day, April 17, 1973, Kateri's feast of her death, Marlene and I were making plans for Peter's upcoming surgery. I asked her a question, and much to my surprise, Peter responded! This was amazing! We had been speaking in normal tones that he couldn't hear. I took Peter to the back of the house, away from noise, covered his ears one at a time and whispered. He could hear me perfectly.

We returned to his physicians, who affirmed that his hearing was completely restored. Peter has perfect hearing, and to this day has not had any recurrence. In fact, he returned to swimming the very day of that doctor's examination and continues to enjoy water sports with not even the slightest of problems since.

Peter recently obtained a Master's Degree in molecular biology and is now a second-year law student at the University of Houston. He plans to combine medicine with law, and is awaiting word on his application to medical school, which he will attend upon graduation from law school. His healing is one of many attributed to Kateri in the depository at the Vatican. We never received official word that it was accepted as a miracle, as one of our doctors refused to cooperate with the Vatican. He believed that medicine prescribed could have been responsible for the healing, however Peter never took that medicine. He hated it and spat it out whenever Marlene tried to give it to him. Dr. Barnett said he had no medical explanation whatsoever for the instant cure. Chronic middle ear problems resulting in deafness do not heal instantly under any circumstances.

In 1980, my family attended the Beatification ceremony for the now Blessed Kateri Tekakwitha. Sitting next to us was a man reading *The Sunday Visitor*. Much to our surprise, Peter's photo was on the front page with the large headline, "Peter Returns to Rome to Thank Kateri!"

We continue lectures on Blessed Kateri and pray for the day that another undisputed miracle is attributed to her intercession, so that she may be known as Saint Kateri Tekakwitha.

Easter In September

John Sumwalt

*The heavens are telling the glory of God; and the
firmament proclaims his handiwork.* (v. 1)

The call came from the doctor that Dad had only a short time
to live. At the age of eighty, after nearly fifty years of farming, this
veteran of World War II was fighting a final battle with Parkinson's
and heart disease.

Daughter Kati and I went ahead of the others and arrived at
the nursing home outside Richland Center at about midnight. Exhausted after the two and half hour drive from Milwaukee, we spent
an hour with Dad and then drove out to the farm to spend the night.
We noticed, as we drove into the yard, that the Easter lily in the
flower garden under the walnut tree was full of buds. Somehow I
knew immediately that the lily would bloom on the day that Dad
died. It was the same lily that had been in Dad's room during the
Easter season. After the blossoms had all dried up, Dad had said,
"Take it to the farm and set it out in the garden; it will bloom again."
I did as he suggested and thought no more about it until I saw the
buds that night.

We spent the following days at Dad's bedside, talking to him
while he was still able, singing his favorite Gospel hymns and praying. Our family took turns being with him through six long days
and nights. Each night, when I returned to the farm to rest, I noticed the buds on the lily were getting heavier and heavier. Finally,
after a long struggle, Dad passed over at about 1:30 p.m. on September 15, 1998.

After a prayer with the pastor and hugs for the nursing home
staff members who had cared for Dad so well, we returned to the
farm with heavy hearts. We saw it before we pulled into the driveway: a glorious white blossom. The first bud had opened. I didn't

know an Easter lily could bloom in September, and I certainly didn't expect it in Wisconsin.

On the day of the funeral there were two more beautiful blossoms. Friends and family from all around the country gathered in the yard on that warm September afternoon, after the funeral service. We sat in a circle under the walnut tree and wondered at this amazing sign of God's presence.

Wisdom From Above

But the wisdom from above is first pure, then peaceable, gentle, willing to yield, full of mercy and good fruits.... (v. 17a)

Martinus Cawley

About fifteen years ago, as I prepared for a big cider-pressing, I had to move the top-heavy hydraulic unit, and I foolishly failed to secure it to the forklift; it toppled over and a key pipe was broken. No one was on hand who knew anything about plumbing, and I foresaw that my own efforts to repair it would take all day. Then I recalled that the man who had helped me the previous year, and who had since died, had been an expert machinist, and had done some plumbing on that machine. With him in mind, I went about the task. It was extremely delicate, but soon I was hearing his voice over my shoulder, "This wrench on that pipe ... a little firmer ... easy does it ... a little more...." Within fifteen minutes, the whole thing was back in working order.

Another time, in the late 1980s, I heard from a nun I had dealt with back in the wild 1960s, when many who, like she and I, had entered religion as teenagers, were discovering how exciting it was to speak freely to members of the opposite sex. She had once again come west for the summer, and wanted to come up and visit. Part of me thought, "To hell with the nonsense of the '60s," while another part felt a frank discussion would be profitable to both of us. The quandary kept coming up in my mind for days, but one day, as I was walking down the road to the farm, I distinctly heard the voice of a saintly and elderly local nun, who had for years given me apples for cider, and who recently had died. Her voice simply said, "I wouldn't if I were you." That settled it. And then, early this year, by a happy Providence, that original nun from the '60s met

144

up with me briefly at a bus station, and we had a delightful little exchange and reconciliation.

Jeanne M. Jones

When we lived in Arizona, my mother-in-law, Frances, lived in the apartment below ours in the house my husband, Maynard, built. He knew of her love for flowers, and built her a greenhouse on two sides of her living room.

One evening, the three of us returned from an outing. As we entered her apartment, prior to going upstairs to ours, both she and I were astounded at the odor of flowers. There were no flowers in bloom in either of our apartments, but she and I could suddenly smell so many flowers it was almost overpowering. Frances told me, "This is what my mother's house smelled like." Maynard couldn't smell a thing, but Frances and I shared that gift of love. I don't know why we were given that particular gift. Who knows, perhaps it was the scent of heaven!

A Narrow Escape

Judy Ziese

We have escaped like a bird from the snare of the
fowlers; the snare is broken, and we have escaped.
Our help is in the name of the Lord, who made
heaven and earth. (vv. 7-8)

When we lived in Dubuque, I often drove down Kennedy Avenue when I went shopping. Kennedy ends abruptly at a stoplight, where it intersects with a major highway. As you approach this intersection you cannot see more than a few yards to the left, because of the hill Kennedy was cut through. One afternoon I was stopped behind another car at this stoplight. I was a bit tired, but watching the light intently. Since I was practicing driving one-footed (I usually use my left for the brake and right for the gas), I was keenly aware of wanting to make a quick response when the light changed. When the change came, the car ahead of me started through the light. When I went to move my foot from the brake to the gas, I felt something pushing down on my knee. I could not move my foot! I looked down at my knee and foot, saw nothing, and then the sensation was gone. Just as my car started to move, a cattle truck roared through the red light from the left. I hit the brakes again and was stunned by the coincidence that had just occurred. I have no doubt that if my leg had not been frozen, either I, the driver behind me, or both of us, would have been in a serious accident. Needless to say, I thanked God for keeping us safe, showing me his presence in such a clear way, and allowing me more time to work on my human/spiritual development.

A Tire Of A Different Dimension

Kay Boone Stewart

Vindicate me, O Lord, for I have walked in my integrity, and I have trusted in the Lord without wavering. Prove me, O Lord, and try me; test my heart and mind. For your steadfast love is before my eyes, and I walk in faithfulness to you. (vv. 1-3)

It was a rainy day in Arizona, and my daughter, Shelley, was on her way to work when a tire on her van blew. Fortunately, she was near the gas station where she stopped routinely. Her van limped into the station. She went into the office, but the usual staff was not there. Just then, a tall, young, blond attendant came through the door, smiling.

"How may I help you?" he asked politely.

"Is there someone here who can change a tire for me? I'm on my way to work and can't wait for an appointment." Just then a man called from the garage, "Hey, Rick!"

Shelley looked at the name stitched on the attendant's shirt pocket, which said *Rick*.

"I'm going to change this lady's tire," he called back.

"Oh, that's another thing. I don't have a spare right now, and I can only afford a used tire. Do you suppose you could find one for me?"

"I don't think we have any used ones right now, but I'll look." He went out to look at her van, taking the tools to change the tire. "What's your name?"

"Shelley. I'm going over to the shopping center to call work," she said, and left. While on the pay phone, she made calls to several other places to see about used tires in the right size, but came up with nothing. When she came back, the tire was changed. To her dismay, and joy, it was a brand new tire.

"Thank you. But I don't have enough money to pay for a new tire today. I'll have to pay on Saturday when I get my paycheck."

"That's fine. However, this is supposed to be your tire."

"What do you mean?"

"I found this tire sitting in the back, all by itself, and this was on it." He showed her a tag with a sticker on one corner where it had been stuck to the tire. It had the name "Shelley" on it.

"I don't understand. I didn't order a tire."

"Nevertheless ... and by the way, we have a special on tires that starts on Saturday."

He wrote up the receipt and handed it to her. She scanned for a price and couldn't find one. There was only a large NC scrawled on the bill.

"But...."

"I told you, this tire was supposed to be yours. I hope the rest of the day goes well."

"Thank you *very* much." She shook her head in disbelief. *If only he knew how really short of money she was!*

She looked back over her shoulder as she left. He waved, smiling. Odd, she thought, I never did see anyone else while I was there, I only heard the voice calling to Rick. She glanced at the bill again. It was signed JC. Why not Rick?

On Saturday, she went back to compliment the young man's service to his boss and to make sure she hadn't taken a tire belonging to some other Shelley. The usual crew were in their places. They recognized her right away.

"I was in last week and got a tire. I wanted to compliment the young man you had on duty. He gave my van excellent service and was very pleasant."

"Who was that?"

"Rick."

"We don't have a Rick working here. You must have been in another station."

"No, I always come here. You know that. I blew a tire right down the street and came in to get it changed." She fished the receipt out of her purse and handed it to the manager. Stamped on the top was their logo and station address.

148

"This says JC. We don't have a JC either."

"He didn't charge me for the tire, and I thought I should come and pay. Also, I thought it might be someone else's tire, since it was sitting by itself and had the name 'Shelley' on it."

"I didn't reserve a tire for anyone. Did you?" he asked his mechanic, who shook his head. Curious now, he went out to look at her tire.

"We don't carry this kind. And I haven't had any of this size in quite a while. You must have been in a different station, Shelley."

"But the receipt has your logo!"

His eyes got a far away look. "What can I tell you? I can't charge you for a tire I don't carry. And no one ordered one of this size."

"Well, thanks!"

He smiled and waved her away. "I didn't do anything."

Her heart sang as she got into the van and drove away. She knew who *did* do something. She had had an angel visitation in the form of Rick, and Jesus Christ had sent him.

We talked it over, later, and decided a time warp had been used on that location where she was a regular customer. Today we would think of it as parallel universes at work. But, whatever the means, the source is our constant — Jesus Christ.

A Sign Of God's Love

Sister Marie Regine Redig

My God, my God, why have you forsaken me? Why are you so far from helping me, from the words of my groaning? O my God, I cry by day, but you do not answer; by night, but find no rest. (vv. 1-2)

I am a member of the School Sisters of Notre Dame. On July 11, 1958, my mother passed away after a year's bout with cancer. Two weeks after her death, I was transferred from Chicago, and a large convent of 33 sisters whom I knew and loved, to a group of four in Morton, Illinois, near Peoria. I didn't know the other three sisters very well. We were starting a new school in a new parish. That was exciting in itself, but I felt holes in the middle of myself. I was 28 years old and this was my first experience of deep, personal grief. I had no idea of what was happening to me, and neither did the other sisters in my community. They were all young, too.

My love for life and fun seemed to be gone. I did my ministry of teaching as best I could, but it didn't energize me in the old way. I mourned my mother every day and missed my family and friends. I wondered what was wrong with me and if I was going a bit crazy. I didn't feel inclined to talk much to the other sisters about it, for fear they would confirm my psychic illness. Oh, if I had only known then what I would learn later: that allowing myself to be vulnerable in sharing and crying, in receiving love and compassion from others, is healing.

Nearly a year went by, and I went off on my annual six-day retreat. I was thoroughly miserable as I looked back over a year that I thought was a total waste. The joy of my religious life and ministry was gone, and I wondered if I would be able to go on.

On about the fourth day of my retreat, I was walking outside in a big field of grass. I was crying and looking down when I saw a

150

tiny flower, no bigger than a quarter of an inch in diameter. Its deep down center was red and the outer edge pink. I can see it as clearly today as then.

My attention was completely absorbed by the flower, and I breathed, "Oh, God, in this vast field, I'm the only one who will ever see this!" Quickly, the answer came back, "Yes, and it's yours, made just for you as a sign of my love." The impact of that moment brings a lump to my throat and tears to my eyes every time I share the story.

That moment did something to my insides. My spirit was touched and I began to feel like my old self, only much richer and wiser with the assurance of God's love.

An Honor Not Taken Lightly

Bruce Stunkard

Every high priest chosen from among mortals is put in charge of things pertaining to God on their behalf, to offer gifts and sacrifices for sins. He is able to deal gently with the ignorant and wayward, since he himself is subject to weakness; and because of this he must offer sacrifice for his own sins as well as for those of the people. And one does not presume to take this honor, but takes it only when called by God, just as Aaron was. (vv. 1-4)

One winter evening, while working in a group home for people with mental disabilities, I took a resident to Saturday evening mass. Her name was Susie. She was a 36-year-old woman with Down's Syndrome. Susie seemed to have two primary interests: eating and hugging. Though eating gave her great pleasure, her food required special preparation, as Susie was missing all of her teeth due to years of dental neglect at a state institution. She also loved to sit down close to a person and hold them for as long as they were willing.

Our activity that evening was church. Neither Susie nor I were Catholic, but St. Alphonsus Church was close, and the early evening service was convenient.

Throughout the Liturgy of the Word, Susie sat close to me, patting my hand as though she were reassuring me that everything would be all right. She passed the time by taking off and putting on her socks and shoes during the Liturgy of the Eucharist. While reciting the Lord's Prayer, she sounded like she was speaking in tongues. We were all invited to pass the peace, however many passed over Susie. As we began to sing, "Lamb of God, you take away the sins of the world," Susie jumped to her feet and we proceeded to the table as the choir sang a Marty Haugen hymn:

Now in this banquet, Christ is our bread; Here shall all
*   hungers be fed.*
Bread that is broken, wine that is poured, Love is the
*   sign of our Lord.*[1]

We arrived at the Banquet table to receive the bread. The priest hesitated slightly when he saw her. He looked at me. I then showed Susie how to cup her hands to receive the Host, and she followed my lead. Taking her action as a sign to proceed, the priest pressed the round white Body of Christ into her palm. Susie looked at it with interest, picked it up with her small right thumb and index finger, and twirled it skillfully, like a magician performing a coin trick. She then handed it back to the priest. From the startled look on his face, I could tell that that had never happened before. His eyes were strained and he again looked to me for help. To relieve the awkwardness, I received Christ's body from her and we recessed back to our place.

Once seated in our pew, thinking the wafer may have been too large for her to chew, I began to break it and spoke the words, "Take and eat, this is my body, broken for you." Then something happened: something that I cannot explain. As I handed her the pieces to eat, the words I had just spoken seemed to reverberate deep within me and began to slowly ascend, until I heard them not in my own voice, but in Susie's. I felt that I was in the presence of Christ, and that I had just fed him. Trembling with awe-filled joy, like Mother Mary I continue to ponder this experience in my heart.

---

1. Marty Haugen, "Now In This Banquet," GIA Publications, 1986.

153

Stopped In Mid-Air

Marjorie K. Evans

This poor soul cried, and was heard by the Lord, and was saved from every trouble. The angel of the Lord encamps around those who fear him, and delivers them. O taste and see that the Lord is good; happy are those who take refuge in him. (vv. 5-8)

It began as a tranquil Sunday afternoon in May. We were in a hurry to get to a Welsh hymn sing at an historic church in an old section of Los Angeles. So, we sped past the once regal Victorian houses, their beauty long since faded.

Suddenly, a young boy, about nine years of age, darted from an overgrown yard into the street. My husband immediately slammed on the brakes, but there was absolutely no way to stop the car before the child would be hit. Horror stricken, I gasped, "Help, Lord!"

Instantly, the boy stopped in mid-stride, as if a giant, unseen hand had reached down and grabbed the collar of his pale, red shirt, and held him immobile. Like a statue he stood there, his body bent slightly forward and his right foot poised in mid-air. He was absolutely motionless, as if riveted to that spot, inches from death, as we slid past him.

After the car skidded to a stop, we got out to see if the child needed help. For a moment or two he remained in suspended animation, a look of bewilderment on his face. Then, shaking his head, he slowly lowered his right foot down to the pavement, turned, and ran back into the yard.

Seizing my husband's hand, I cried, " 'For he will command his angels concerning you ... on their hands they will bear you up ...' (Psalm 91:11-12). Honey, we've just witnessed a miracle!"

Our Family In Heaven

Jeff Veenhuis

*And I heard a loud voice from the throne saying,
"See, the home of God is among mortals. He will
dwell with them; they will be his peoples, and God
himself will be with them, he will wipe away every
tear from their eyes." (vv. 3-4a)*

Our daughter, Nicole, was born November 16, 1998, a beautiful and apparently healthy baby. Betsy and I were elated. Several days later, our dreams and aspirations for a healthy first child, and our parents' first grandchild, came crashing down. Nicole had a hypoplastic left heart, which means she was born with only one of the two pumping chambers, or ventricles, in her heart. She also had what the doctors called "transposition of the greater vessels." Her aorta and pulmonary artery were transposed. The doctors did everything they could to save Nicole, but her heart could not support her tiny body. She passed away on November 24, at the age of eight days.

Betsy and I, and all of our family, were devastated. It was the most difficult and soul searching event in our lives. It has been a challenge to our faith. We have wondered why God would want to take a seemingly perfect child from us.

Six months later, in May of 1999, we were still wondering, when I had a startling dream which caused me to sit bolt upright in bed and to begin sweating profusely. The dream involved a message from two very important men in my life, my own dear grandfather, Clarence Eisenga, and Betsy's grandfather, Harold Bergman, a man I had never met.

Grandpa Eisenga was a large man, with a big heart, whose weathered body showed many signs of his almost seventy years of farming. His posture and pose were impressive. His hands and feet were huge. I will never forget being enveloped in his enormous lap and the safety it provided throughout my childhood and much of my adolescence. Grandpa was a devoutly Christian man who often spoke, with a tear in his eye, of the importance of family and of the absolute necessity of a Christian home. He was very proud of his family, especially all of his grandchildren and great-grandchildren. Grandpa became ill shortly after Nicole died and went to heaven in March of 1999.

It seemed very natural, that night, to find myself sitting again in Grandpa's big, comfortable lap. I saw a bright round light, and in its shadow, on one side, the well-lit image of Harold Bergman, the man I had never met; Betsy's grandfather who died in 1986, long before she and I had even dated.

I had seen many pictures of Harold. He was a strapping man who loved people and revelled in the sales work he did for the family paper company. Like my grandfather, Harold loved God and he adored his family. All of his grandchildren referred to him fondly as "Bumpa." He was a longtime active member of Wauwatosa Avenue United Methodist Church, where Betsy and I are now members. I always wished that I had met him and been able to know him.

Harold was holding a baby girl in his arms. He was looking down in fondness at the baby and never really looked up at me until the very end of the dream. I remember gazing down and seeing Grandpa Eisenga's work jeans. I never saw his face, but I felt the unmistakable presence of his lap. I know I was in Grandpa's lap, because I heard his deep, somewhat slurred voice reassure me, saying only, "We are just fine." While it seems disconnected, all I remember next is looking at the bright, round light, now with Grandpa's back to me, silhouetted against it. As he walked closer to Harold and the baby, Harold passed the baby into Grandpa's arms, and then Harold spoke to me for the first time ever. While I cannot describe the sound of his voice, or exactly what he said, I know I will hear him again one day and I will know him instantly. He said something to the effect, "Like you and Betsy are a family, we too are a family here. We love you very much."

156

Call me clueless, but until he said that, it had not hit me that the baby was Nicole. This discovery startled me and I awoke. I found myself sitting upright in bed, something that has never happened to me before or since, and I immediately started to sweat. It must have been about 1 a.m. I remember lying awake for over an hour, trying to make sense out of what I had seen and heard.

Was there a message I was supposed to receive from this "vision"? The images and tones in my vision were not soft, as one might expect, but very sharp and clear. The message was clear, too, that we should always remember that we have family in heaven, caring for those who go before us, and that our family on earth carries over into heaven. I believe that Harold taught Nicole and Grandpa Eisenga how to "touch" people on earth. He has always been described to me as a "people person" while he was on earth, and has seemingly remained active in the afterlife. Harold appeared several times to family and friends while we lived in his former house in Wauwatosa. I think he and Grandpa wanted to let us know that all is right in heaven by reinforcing the tie between earthly and heavenly families.

These men were father figures in many people's lives while they were here, and were the patriarchs of their families. Their values and their compassion are instilled in each of those they left behind. Someday, I, too, will be a patriarch. I have these men and their legacy to maintain and uphold.

There are many things I have learned and been forced to think through after Nicole's and Grandpa's deaths. This vision is sure to bring new meaning as I continue to understand its message.

Christ Entered In

Patricia Lietzke

*But when Christ came as a high priest of the good
things that have come, then through the greater
and perfect tent (not made with hands, that is, not
of this creation), he entered once for all into the
Holy Place, not with the blood of goats and calves,
but with his own blood, thus obtaining eternal re-
demption.* (vv. 11-12)

In November of 1989, during a time away from home for personal spiritual growth, I had a short dream. The memory of it, even
today, is clear and simple. The dream left me with the image of an
old, balding man, head slightly bowed, who was facing away from
me. His attire was an oversized coat and slacks that drooped in
folds over his shoes.

During the day, the image remained in my mind's eye, and I
was puzzled by it, wondering whether I might be able to draw the
man. I knew I could draw what I see with my eyes, so I thought I
might do that with the mind's eye image as well, and it proved to
be quite easy.

I shared the art rendition and dream with a friend who suggested that I prop the picture at my bedside before I slept, inviting
the old man to "tell" me what he wanted, and why he had come in
my dream. I followed the suggestion out of curiosity.

That night, I felt awakened by the window being rattled in the
wind of a snowstorm. I was not fully awake or asleep. It was as if
I was semi-conscious. The image of the old man was clear in the
night, even though I could not actually see the drawing in the darkness. I asked the man to tell me what he wanted. His answer was,
"Take Christ into yourself." At that point, I found myself, still only
semi-conscious, drawing my hands over my body from my pelvic

area up to my chest, repeating the motion for a very long time until I fell soundly asleep.

In the morning, I felt surprised and a little overwhelmed by the experience. I commented to others during the morning about the windy, stormy night, and was greeted by quizzical looks and comments about the stillness of the night.

The next day, I drew the profile of a woman looking up with the appearance of "knowing" or "understanding." A few weeks later, I drew another image that seemed to be connected to the first two. It was a figure in a cape with hands reaching out in front that had yellow bursts of energy coming from them. The three images became for me "spirit guides" who represent pain, wisdom, and healing.

Until now, I have only shared this event with a few trusted friends. The experience has kept me on the path of my Christian faith and its roots. Christ's life and teachings are those, for me, that I attempt to example as best I can through my life. I feel that the dream images are gifts to be treasured from a loving creator.

Eagerly Waiting

And just as it is appointed for mortals to die once,
and after that the judgment, so Christ, having been
offered once to bear the sins of many, will appear a
second time, not to deal with sin, but to save those
who are eagerly waiting for him. (v. 27)

Eileen Fink

In my dream, I was in my bed trying to get to sleep when I heard someone coming. My heart was in my throat and I was filled with fear as he came closer. I thought, "I'll pretend I'm sleeping and maybe he'll go away." Then I heard my husband's voice saying, "I'll be coming for you soon." The fear disappeared and when I turned to see him, I awoke. I lay there feeling such happiness and peace. It was so good to hear his voice! He's been gone for almost nine years.

Pamela Burns

Some years ago, when I worked as a registered nurse in a nursing home, I knew a delightful Polish woman whose sweet personality was apparent to everyone even though she spoke no English. Her daughter came every day to bring her dinner and to eat with her. The daughter told us her mother had been a Polish Freedom Fighter, and because of this she and her mother had been incarcerated in a Nazi concentration camp. The daughter told how her mother had suffered and sacrificed in many ways to keep her alive.

One evening, the mother and her daughter and I were watching the evening news as I finished my rounds. We watched in amazement as the Berlin wall was being torn down. None of us could take our eyes off of the television, especially the old woman. When the news was over we looked over at her and she was still. The old freedom fighter had quietly passed.

A Deep Peace

Jodie and Georgia N. Hunt

Let us hold fast to the confession of our hope with-
out wavering, for he who has promised is faithful.
(v. 24)

My father died suddenly, at the age of 58, while he was on business in Canada. I felt badly that my siblings and I had not had a chance to say good-bye, and it troubled me very deeply that he died alone, without family and friends around him. We were all very close to him. One day I was vacuuming and I smelled pipe tobacco very strongly (my father was a pipe smoker), so strongly that it stopped me short. I had to stop and look around and see. I realized he came to tell me it was okay and that I could let go. I felt a deep peace after that.

About a week later, I received the following note from my daughter, Georgia, as a P.S. in a birthday card. I had not told her about my experience:

Dear Mom,

I know that you wish your father could still be here with you. I know you will always have his presence in your heart. I truly believe that he is here with us in spirit. Last night, I went downstairs to find a picture of a daffodil in the encyclopedia, and I felt a strong presence with me. I looked around to see if you or Dad had come downstairs, because I thought for sure someone was around. But I didn't see anyone. I got this strange, overpowering feeling in my heart — and for a few minutes I felt so content and safe. The strange thing is, I smelled pipe tobacco. It's weird how much I had forgotten that wonderful smell. Well, anyway, I knew that Grandpa's spirit was in that room with me. I thought of you and tears came to my eyes. I thought I should share this whole thing with you. You are as special to me as your father is to you.

Reaping Joy

Jo Perry-Sumwalt

May those who sow in tears reap with shouts of joy. Those who go out weeping, bearing the seed for sowing, shall come home with shouts of joy, carrying their sheaves. (vv. 5-6)

When I was thirteen, my maternal grandfather died very suddenly. It was a great shock to my whole family. In the days before small towns such as mine had EMT's and ambulances, it was the undertaker who responded to the need for emergency transport to the nearest hospital. Needless to say, an undertaker is not trained in speed and efficiency in caring for the dying, only the dead. My grandfather, suffering from a major heart attack, didn't survive the trip to the hospital.

Being thirteen, with all of the normal hormonal peaks and valleys ravaging my life, I took Grandpa's death very hard. His is not the first I remember in my family; I had attended funerals for a little second cousin and an uncle by marriage. But his was the most personal. At that time in my life, churchgoer though I was, I felt crushed by the loss. I felt abandoned by both Grandpa and God.

As a result of seeing his death as a personal affront, I refused to attend my grandfather's wake. My parents, brother, and sisters pleaded with me to reconsider, but I was very sure that I did not want to see my grandfather laid out in a casket with a whole lot of people around. I insisted that I wanted to remember him as I had last seen him: alive, a little loud, laughing. However, I did agree that I would go to the funeral, as long as the casket was closed.

We all made it through the funeral, the burial in my hometown cemetery, and the funeral lunch with our whole family and many friends and neighbors. Everyone helped look after Grandma, who was also devastated, and time began to heal the wound. But I never stopped taking Grandpa's death personally. I had a "thing" about funerals after that, and I never really let go of the hurt.

After I had completed high school and beauty culture training, and was out on my own, I had a dream one night. I don't remember any circumstances surrounding that time, except that I was sharing an apartment with two beauty school friends and trying to make a living. There was no reason that I can think of for this dream to have happened at that particular time: no traumas, no deaths, no yearnings. But one night, out of nowhere, Grandpa came to me in a dream. He told me he was okay. He looked good, like I had wanted to remember him: alive, a little loud, laughing. Grandpa told me not to be sad for him anymore, and he assured me that everything would be all right. I woke up from that dream smiling, comforted and happy. I couldn't wait to tell my mom, and have her tell Grandma, that I was certain Grandpa was okay.

My grandfather's visit not only reassured me that he was taken care of, it changed my concept of death. I no longer doubt that those who die are alive, not just in our hearts, but indeed, with God. I'm forever grateful for that dream. Grandpa's visit was a reassurance of what is to come for all of us.

Seeing Jesus

*Look! He is coming with the clouds; every eye will
see him....* (v. 7a)

Lee Meissner

It was a nice summer day. A mother and her two children,
Marilyn and Gerry, were in the family car heading home after doing the weekly shopping. Everything was very routine. They had
made the trip a thousand times. Then it happened. A car driven by
a teenage boy didn't stop for a stop sign. The car with the mother
and the children had the right of way. They were just in the wrong
place at the wrong time.

The car that went through the stop sign couldn't have stopped.
The police later estimated that the car was traveling at excess of
ninety miles per hour. The impact was almost unimaginable. The
children went through the roof of the car (this was in the days be
fore seatbelts). The mother was near death, with many internal injuries and a broken neck, and in a coma.

A funeral was held for the children. The father didn't know
how he would tell his wife that their children had been killed when
she regained consciousness, if in fact she ever did.

It was about two weeks later that she came out of the coma.
Now it was time to tell her that the children were gone. Her husband tried to tell her, but before he could get the words out she
said, "I know Marilyn and Gerry are gone, but it's okay. I saw
them here in my room. They were sitting on my bed and Jesus was
with them. He was holding them. I know they will be all right."

In time the mother recovered from her injuries. Although she
did have some neck problems later in life, it was nothing that kept
her from doing what she wanted to do. The couple later took in
foster children, some short-term and some long-term.

This accident occurred in 1948 or 1949. The couple were my wife Helen's foster parents. She was placed in their care at the age of thirteen and lived with them until she went to college.

Paul Tulppo

Back in 1946, when I was eight years old, I was returning from a day in the woods on the far west side of Detroit with my friend Jim, who was my age, and his brother Anthony, who was two years older. As we headed toward home, the brothers suggested that we stop at their church, so they could show me, a non-Catholic, how they blessed themselves with holy water when they entered the church.

I followed them into their church, we all put our fingers into the holy water, and they crossed themselves. Then we knelt in the very last pew. When we looked up, we saw the Lord Jesus Christ standing on the altar, about 25 feet away. His arms were outstretched and there was a beautiful glow completely surrounding him. The three of us were in complete awe. We jumped to our feet and ran out of the church, and we didn't stop running until we reached home and told our mothers what we had seen.

I remember that vision as though it happened five minutes ago.

Perhaps only in our mystical moments do we know what is really happening in our lives.

Thomas Moore

This is a first in a series of three books of mystical stories. If you have a story to share, please send it to John Sumwalt at 2044 Forest Street, Wauwatosa, Wisconsin 53213, or fax to 414-453-0702, or e-mail to jsumwalt@naspa.net. Phone 414-257-1228.

Thomas Moore, *Original Self: Living With Paradox and Originality* (New York: HarperCollins, 2000), p. 133.

Contributors

Theonia Amenda is a retired Diaconal Minister in The United Methodist Church. She continues in ministry in the area of Spiritual Formation as the leader of a Three Year Covenant Community and as a spiritual director. Write to her at: 3612 Birnamwood Drive, Slinger, Wisconsin 53086. Phone: 262-644-8385.

Janet Angel, Ph.D., has been active in the field of natural health and healing for over fifteen years. She is a motivational and inspirational speaker, counselor, composer and spiritual leader who has appeared as a guest on many radio programs. Janet is the author of *All That You Are — Your True Identity,* the first in a series of books. Contact her at janetangel@home.com or her website: www.JanetAngel.com or phone her at 847-705-3861. Write to: 800 E. Northwest Hwy. Suite 700, Palatine, Illinois 60074.

Bonny J. Bailey is a member of Christ United Methodist Church in Greenfield, Wisconsin, where she leads a group called Companions In Christ. She is also a part of a Three Year Covenant Community and has been involved in many Bible study classes. She has published poems and loves to write. Bonny is retired and has been happily remarried for many years.

Kay L. Bandle lives in West Bend, Wisconsin, with her husband Fred and daughter, Jessica Bobholz. Kay works as a dental hygienist and enjoys spending time with her family. She is a writer, dedicated to sharing her love for God with others. E-mail: FBKLBJLB@peoplepc.com

Christal Bindrich is a United Methodist pastor at Mayville United Methodist Church in Mayville, Wisconsin. She welcomes opportunities to talk about mystical experiences. She can be reached at 307 N. Main Street, Mayville, Wisconsin 53050. Phone: 920-387-4711. E-mail: bindrich@internetwis.com

169

Margaret Nyland-Brown lives in Milwaukee with her husband and their pets. She is a two-time graduate of the University of Wisconsin-Milwaukee in Psychology (BA 1992) and dance (BFA w/honors 1999). She works as a choreographer and coach for figure skaters.

Pamela Burns is a Christian through the prayers of many at the age of fifteen. Since then she has been shown the workings of God in small and large ways. Pamela is a mother, wife, RN, and BSN in Milwaukee, Wisconsin.

Martinus Cawley left Austrailia at seventeen to become a Trappist. He studied in Rome and Jerusalem. His monastic day includes bookbinding, harvest-gleaning, recycling, translating, writing, and printing biographical and descriptive texts from the abbey's multiple heritage. Write to him at Guadalupe Abbey, Lafayette, Oregon 97127. Phone: 503-852-7174. Fax: 503-852-7748. E-mail: martinus@trappistabbey.org

Todd Chrisler received his B.A. degree in Criminal Justice from Concordia University . He manages a Pizza Hut and attends Faith Lutheran Church in Cedarburg, Wisconsin. Phone: 262-993-1000.

John W. Doll began writing lyrics in Chicago for Lawrence Welk. Before his retirement in 1987, he did marketing for one of Time Mirror's Corporations. He is a freelance writer with stories published in a number of anthologies, including the *Chicken Soup For The Soul* series and Cheryl Kirking's recent book, *Ripples of Joy*. He lives in the middle of a 25-acre orange grove with his wife Lanie. He can be reached at 2377 Grand Avenue, Fillmore, California 93015. Phone: 805-524-3821.

William L. Dow is a Licensed Local Pastor serving the Amherst and Buena Vista United Methodist Churches in the Wisconsin Annual Conference. He is the owner-operator of a Laser Engineering and Cutting Business. He has also worked as a High School Industrial Technology Teacher, and for many years as a trainer in the quality improvement process for a Fortune 500 Company. Write to him at: W3008 49th Street, Mauston, Wisconsin 53948. Phone: 608-847-2398. E-mail: bandrdow@mwt.net

Vickie Eckoldt is a member of Wauwatosa Avenue United Methodist Church in Milwaukee, Wisconsin. With the help of her pastor, she decided to share her story with the hope that it might inspire others faced with a similar situation never to give up.

Edgar A. Evans, a retired accountant and office manager, is now a freelance writer with several published articles. He and his wife, Marjorie, are members of Pacific Church of Irvine, California. Write to him at: 4162 Fireside Circle, Irvine, California 92604.

Marjorie K. Evans, a former elementary school teacher, is now a freelance writer with many published articles and stories including the *Chicken Soup For The Soul* series. She and her husband, Edgar, are members of Pacific Church of Irvine, California. She enjoys their two sons, their daughter-in-law, and five grandchildren. Write to her at: 4162 Fireside Circle, Irvine, California 92604.

Keith R. Eytcheson, Sr., retired from the USAF on March 1, 1970, after 22 years of service. He was appointed as a Local Pastor in 1991 and served First United Methodist Church in Genoa City, as associate Pastor at Lake Geneva UMC and Interim Pastor at Community UMC in Waterford, Wisconsin. He is now fully retired and preaches occasionally. E-mail: keith@genevaonline.com

Eileen Fink attends Spring Lake Community Church in Green Bay, Wisconsin.

Robert L. Gossett is pastor of Grand Avenue United Methodist Church in Port Washington, Wisconsin, where he lives with his wife Jeri. They have two grown children, Tim and Christina. Bob has had several articles published in *Marriage* magazine. Fax: 262-284-9478. E-mail: gaumc@milwpc.com

171

Rebecca Henderleiter is a Native American Catholic and attends the Congregation of the Great Spirit in Milwaukee, Wisconsin. She is a recovering addict, clean since 1989. Her life is devoted to her sons, Tony and Matthew, and to working with addicts and mentally ill persons seeking recovery. E-mail: henderleiter@cs.com

Lori Hetzel has been happily married to her best friend for thirteen years. They have two sons, Logan, 12, and Connor Dane, 6. She works as a dental assistant and is a member of Christ United Methodist Church in Greenfield, Wisconsin.
E-mail: LJHetzel@wi.rr.com

Jean Hodge is a member of West Bend Calvary Assembly of God Church in West Bend, Wisconsin. She is a certified minister of the Assembly of God Church. Jean preached and taught Sunday school for over 25 years. Still active for the Lord at the age of ninety, she spends time in prayer each day for her family and beloved church.

Georgia Nicole Hunt was born in Brookfield, and grew up in Wauwatosa, Wisconsin. She attends school at Montana State University and plans to be a teacher. She enjoys skiing and hiking.

Jodie Hunt is Church Administrator and long time member of Wauwatosa Avenue United Methodist Church in Wauwatosa, Wisconsin. She has served as an officer and chair of many church and community groups. Jodie and her husband, Jeff, have been married for 25 years and have two grown children, Georgia and Aaron.

Judie M. Jacobson is a pastor, retreat leader, poet, writer, quilter, gourmet cook, and water color artist. She is a naturalist who loves tent camping, canoeing, and hiking. Judie has two grown children and two grandsons who are pure "joy." Write to her at: 516 W. Indian Hills Drive, Waterloo, Wisconsin. Phone: 920-478-9523. E-mail: UMC@hurleycomputers.com

Susan D. Jamison is an ordained elder in the Central Pennsylvania Conference of The United Methodist Church. In addition to serving in parish ministry, she has worked as a counselor with survivors of abuse and as a parent educator. E-mail: sjamison@evenlink.net

Jeanne M. Jones is pastor of Willow Valley and Ash Creek United Methodist Churches near Richland Center, Wisconsin. Write to her at: P.O. Box 153, Sextonville, Wisconsin 53584. E-mail: paradigm@mwt.net

Earl Kammerud was ordained as an elder in the Wisconsin Conference of The United Methodist Church in 1971, and serves as pastor of Central United Methodist Church in Milwaukee. Phone: 414-344-1600.

Sandra Kilbride-Becker is a member of Trinity United Methodist Church in Montello, Wisconsin.

Elaine H. Klemm-Grau is a retired Psychotherapist, MSSW, UWM, Spiritual Director, MA, Sacred Heart School of Theology, Hales Corners, Wisconsin, Sacred Heart Congregation, Racine, Wisconsin, Eucharistic Minister, Catechist, Lector, Communion Presider and President of Hickory Hollow Development. Contact her at: 4835 Richmond Drive, Racine, Wisconsin 53406. Phone: 262-637-2277. E-mail: egrau@execpc.com

Dorothy Kraemer was a long-time member of Wauwatosa Avenue United Methodist Church. Her story was read at her memorial service at the church on September 1, 1995. It first appeared in *Lectionary Tales For The Pulpit*, John Sumwalt & Jo Perry Sumwalt, CSS Publishing Company, 1996, pp. 108-111.

Diana Lampsa, M.D., is a psychiatrist and owner of Great Lakes Psychiatric Center in Manitowoc, Wisconsin. She is a member of Zion United Methodist Church in Mishicot and an occasional contributor to *The Wisconsin Psychiatrist.* Diana is co-founder of the Brain Foundation, a non-profit organization advancing public education regarding mental illness. Write to her at: Box 400, Manitowoc, Wisconsin 54221. E-mail: dlampsa@powerweb.net

Marcia Lee, a semi-retired accountant, now spends most of her time doing volunteer work. She is Eucharistic Minister to the sick, a spiritual director, and member of St. James Catholic Church. Write to her at: 11428 Susan Lane, McMinnville, Oregon 97128. Phone: 503-434-6641.

Patricia L. Lietzke works as a multimedia artist with a focus on touch drawing. She has an art studio/gallery called "Leap of Faith" and worships at Community United Methodist Church in Cedarburg, Wisconsin.

Kenneth Lyerly is a Local Pastor serving United Methodist Churches in Genoa City and Pleasant Prairie, Wisconsin. Write to him at: 7937 30th Avenue, Kenosha, Wisconsin 53142. Phone: 262-694-1468. E-mail: klyerly@wi.rr.com

Dr. Robert Maeglin worked for thirty years as a scientist at the U.S. Forest Products Laboratory. He retired in 1989 to become a Licensed Local Pastor in the United Methodist Church. He serves the Lime Ridge and Sandusky United Methodist Churches in rural Sauk County, Wisconsin. Dr. Maeglin is author of over sixty scientific and technical articles, as well as numerous conservation articles. E-mail: reimeyer@merr.com

Patricia Gallagher Marchant is a Family Therapist in private practice in Milwaukee, Wisconsin. She is a member of Our Lady of Lourdes Catholic Church. Patricia can be reached at: 414-224-0800 or E-mail: marchant@execpc.com

Allan and Marlene McCauley live in Phoenix, Arizona, where Allan has practiced trial law for thirty years. Marlene is an artist and the author of *Adventures With A Saint ... Kateri Tekakwitha, Lily of the Mohawks,* and *Whitey From Heaven ... a Wondrous Cat.* Both of them lecture on Kateri. As an avocation, they and their six children did puppet shows all over the U.S. for many years as the "McCauley Family Theatre." Phone: 602-265-9151.

Kai Monique McClinton is pastor of Solomon Community Temple in Milwaukee. Write to her at: 3295 N. Martin Luther King Drive, Milwaukee, Wisconsin 53212. Phone: 414-372-2101. E-mail: revkaimcclinton1@juno.com

Lee E. Meissner is pastor of Christ United Methodist Church of Watertown, Wisconsin, and has served United Methodist churches since 1976. He received his Master of Divinity and MAR degrees from the University of Dubuque Theological Seminary in Dubuque, Iowa.

Lynette Ellis Metz was transplanted from Virginia to Wisconsin after she married her husband, Paul. After the births of their five children, she graduated from Mount Mary College with degrees in behavioral science and theology. Besides God and family, Lynette's true love is youth ministry. Write to her at: W127 N14185 Marquette Road, Richfield, Wisconsin 53076. E-mail: twometz@nconnect.net

Ena Minckler has taught Sunday school at West Allis Wesleyan Church in West Allis, Wisconsin, for over 35 years. She served as treasurer for 27 years.

Roy H. Nelson is an attorney, mediator, arbitrator, and Certified Christian Conciliator. He speaks frequently on resolving conflict biblically. He is a member of St. Matthew's Lutheran Church, Wauwatosa, Wisconsin, and is preparing to enter seminary. E-mail: RHNMGN@aol.com

Iris Ninis is affiliated with Christ United Methodist Church in Greenfield, Wisconsin. She is a Wisconsin State Registered Massage Therapist. Iris is the author of a collection of sacred poetry and prayers titled, *And Your Life Will Sing*. Write to her at: P.O. Box 270272, Milwaukee, Wisconsin 53227 Phone: 414-416-2632.

Rochelle Pennington has worked as both a writer and consultant with Jack Canfield *(Chicken Soup for the Soul)*, H. Jackson Brown *(Life's Little Instruction Book)*, and Alice Gray *(Stories For the*

Heart). Her book, *Highlighted In Yellow,* was released in 2001. She writes a weekly newspaper column, and has also written stories, articles, and dramas for numerous anthologies, magazines, and playwright publications. She can be reached by writing: N3535 Corpus Christi, Campbellsport, Wisconsin 53010.

Jo Perry-Sumwalt is Director of Christian Education at Wauwatosa Avenue United Methodist Church. She has co-authored two books with her husband, John, *Life Stories,* '95, and *Lectionary Tales For The Pulpit,* '96. Besides John, writing, and their two grown children, Kati and Orrin, Jo's loves are needlework, furniture refinishing, antiquing, refurbishing their farm house, long walks with John, and their seven-year-old Westie, Eli.
E-mail: jsumwalt@naspa.net

Ann Watson Peterson is working on a Master of Divinity degree at Garret-Evangelical Seminary in Evanston, Illinois. She is the mother of three and stepmother of three. Ann is a member of the United Methodist Church of Whitefish Bay, where she serves on the Prayer Ministry Team and helps coordinate the Saturday Family Worship service. She has written numerous articles for Mount Mary College publications and is working on an article for *Milwaukee Magazine.* E-mail: awp521@aol.com

Marie Regine Redig, SSND, ministers as the coordinator of the Euens Spirituality Center at Mount Mary College and does individual retreat and spiritual direction. She is a member of Mary Queen of Martyrs Roman Catholic Church. Write to her at: 4244 N. 50th Street, Milwaukee, Wisconsin 53216-1313. Phone: 414-445-9642. E-mail: rredig@ssnd-milw.org

Loxley Ann Schlosser has been married to Jim for 22 years, and is the mother of Kimberly and Kristine and grandmother of Kendra, Cheyenne, and Sierra. She is a fulltime secretary at Brookfield Academy and part-time shift manager at Four Seasons Coffee in Brookfield, Wisconsin. She is a member of Community Church in West Bend, Wisconsin.

Ruth A. Smith grew up on a dairy farm in Wisconsin and never makes the same recipe twice. She has lived in six different states and China. Ruth is a substitute teacher and loves working with children. She and her husband Bruce operate a home-based business in Sheboygan, Wisconsin, selling old non-fiction books on the Internet. Look for them on eBay.com, seller name, *chinasmith*. They specialize in history and reference books. Bruce is writing a book listing Missouri tokens and collects old checks, paper items, postcards, and anything to do with Missouri banking history. E-mail: smithbr@bytehead.com

Manda R. Stack is an ordained minister in The United Church of Christ. She serves as pastor of Raymond Community Church, UCC, and Union Grove Congregational Church in southeast Wisconsin. She can be reached by E-mail: manda@wi.net

Kay Boone Stewart is a novelist (*Trilogy, Chariots of Dawn*, E. Thomas Nelson '92), poet (*Sunrise Over Galilee* '93, *The Color Red*, '94), non-fiction books (*Here's Help*, '93, Collaborator, *Don Stewart Tips...*'93, *Window Watchman 11*, CIN '97), artist (Kay Cards-2001), music composer, harpist, vocalist, storyteller, Member/deacon Presbyterian Church, *Who's Who/American Women* (2000), *Who's Who America* (2002). She can be reached at: P.O. Box 727, Brentwood, California 94513. E-mail: KSB@mailbox.com

Bruce Stunkard is a circuit-riding United Methodist preacher serving Ellsworth, Hartland, and Diamond Bluff United Methodist Churches in northwestern Wisconsin. He is married and has two children. Bruce is a teacher of the Enneagram and enjoys woodworking, kayaking, searching for stones, and Lake Superior. Write to him at: 520 River Hills Drive, River Falls, Wisconsin 54022. Phone: 715-425-1196. E-mail: brucestunkard@mediaone.net

John Sumwalt is pastor of Wauwatosa Avenue United Methodist Church. He is the author of the best-selling CSS series, *Lectionary Stories*, '90, '91, and '92. John has co-authored two books with his wife Jo, *Life Stories,* '95 and *Lectionary Tales For The Pulpit,*

'96. He does storytelling, inspirational speaking, and retreats. Write to John at: 2044 Forest Street, Milwaukee, Wisconsin 53213. Phone: 414-257-1228. Fax: 414-453-0702. E-mail: jsumwalt@naspa.net

Kathryn Taughinbaugh is a sophmore at Rufus King High School in Milwaukee. She is a leader in the Youth Fellowship group at Wauwatosa Avenue United Methodist Church and serves on the design team for Convo, an annual convocation for United Methodist Youth in Wisconsin.

Patricia Marie Thaker is a graduate student and registered nurse at the University of Wisconsin's Pediatric Intensive Care Unit in Madison. She was married on August 11, 2001, to Alejandro Rivera in Milwaukee.

Rosmarie Trapp is a member of the "Community of the Crucified One," 104 E. 11th Avenue, Homestead, Pennsylvania 15120. Rosmarie lives in an apartment in one of their mission houses in Vermont, where she is involved in children's Bible classes, fund raisers, and prison ministry, sharing that "Jesus loves you." Her family's story was told in the well-known movie, *The Sound of Music*.

Paul Tulppo is a member of Christ United Methodist Church in Greenfield, Wisconsin. He served as a machinist in the U.S. Navy for 31 years. Paul and his wife, Dorothy Jean, enjoy their son, two daughters, six grandchildren, and five great-grandchildren. Phone: 414-281-9187. E-mail: PTULPPO@AOL.COM

Jeff Veenhuis resides in Brookfield, Wisconsin, with his wife Betsy and their two-year-old son Jacob. He works for Medtronics, a leading Medical Device Technology Company. He is a member of Wauwatosa Avenue United Methodist Church. E-mail: jveenhuis@sofamordanek.com

Judy Von Bergen is a member of Covenant Presbyterian Church in Madison, Wisconsin. She previously had a story published in

Uplift, a book by and for breast cancer survivors. Judy recently retired from the resale business after twenty years as a shop owner.

Wendy Wosoba is a retired elementary teacher, wife, mother of two, and grandmother of two. She is a member Perseverance Presbyterian Church in Milwaukee, where she serves as an elder. Wendy enjoys teaching adults and children. E-mail: rwosoba@msn.com

Judy Ziese is married and the mother of two grown children. She works as a Respite Coordinator for a non-profit organization in Stevens Point, Wisconsin. E-mail: jezmund@coredcs.com

John Zingaro is pastor of Bryn Mawr Presbyterian Church in the Madison suburb of Cottage Grove, Wisconsin. A native of Pennsylvania, he has served in Africa as a missionary, teaching English in Tanzania, and has lived in Germany and England. He is the author of two books: *Thielemann, the Preacher's Preacher* and *Harry Potter Sermons*. Write to him at: P.O. Box 236 Cottage Grove, Wisconsin 53527. Phone: 608-839-4768.
E-mail: jzingaro@mailbag.com